It's All about the Woman Who Wears It
Cristina Pérez
646.70082

IT'S ALL ABOUT THE
WOMAN WHO
WEARS IT

IT'S ALL ABOUT THE WOMAN WHO WEARS IT

10 Laws
for Being
Smart,
Successful,
and *Sexy*
Too

Two-Time Emmy Award–Winning Television Judge
CRISTINA PEREZ

A CELEBRA BOOK

CELEBRA
Published by New American Library, a division of
Penguin Group (USA) Inc., 375 Hudson Street,
New York, New York 10014, USA
Penguin Group (Canada), 90 Eglinton Avenue East, Suite 700, Toronto,
Ontario M4P 2Y3, Canada (a division of Pearson Penguin Canada Inc.)
Penguin Books Ltd., 80 Strand, London WC2R 0RL, England
Penguin Ireland, 25 St. Stephen's Green, Dublin 2,
Ireland (a division of Penguin Books Ltd.)
Penguin Group (Australia), 250 Camberwell Road, Camberwell, Victoria 3124,
Australia (a division of Pearson Australia Group Pty. Ltd.)
Penguin Books India Pvt. Ltd., 11 Community Centre, Panchsheel Park,
New Delhi - 110 017, India
Penguin Group (NZ), 67 Apollo Drive, Rosedale, North Shore 0632,
New Zealand (a division of Pearson New Zealand Ltd.)
Penguin Books (South Africa) (Pty.) Ltd., 24 Sturdee Avenue,
Rosebank, Johannesburg 2196, South Africa

Penguin Books Ltd., Registered Offices:
80 Strand, London WC2R 0RL, England

First published by Celebra,
a division of Penguin Group (USA) Inc.

First Printing, March 2010
10 9 8 7 6 5 4 3 2 1

Copyright © Cristina Perez, 2010
All rights reserved

CELEBRA and logo are trademarks of Penguin Group (USA) Inc.

Library of Congress Cataloging-in-Publication Data:

Perez, Cristina.
    It's all about the woman who wears it: 10 laws for being smart, successful, and sexy too/
Cristina Perez.
        p. cm.
    ISBN 978-0-451-22949-6
    1. Women—Life skills guides.   2. Women—Conduct of life.   3. Women—Psychology.
I. Title.
    HQ1221.P43   2010
    646.70082—dc22   2009040446

Set in Adobe Garamond
Designed by Spring Hoteling

Printed in the United States of America

I dedicate this book to my husband, Christopher.
The only man who drives me crazy in every sense of the word.

Contents

PART I: *Introduction*   1

PART II: *Identifying with Yourself*   13

CHAPTER 1: **Law #1**—*Find Strength in Yourself*   15

CHAPTER 2: **Law #2**—*Celebrate Being a Woman*   55

CHAPTER 3: **Law #3**—*Take a Risk*   79

PART III: *Identifying with Others*   93

CHAPTER 4: **Law #4**—*Date Wisely*   95

CHAPTER 5: **Law #5**—*Understand the Rules of Engagement*   125

CHAPTER 6: **Law #6**—*Avoid the Seven Deadly Sins of Marriage*   141

CHAPTER 7: **Law #7**—*Be Smart and Successful in Friendship*   169

PART IV: *Identifying with Life*   189

CHAPTER 8: **Law #8**—*Master the Balancing Act*   191

CHAPTER 9: **Law #9**—*Reinvent Yourself*   211

CHAPTER 10: **Law #10**—*Live with It*   225

PART V: *Conclusion: The Empowered Identity*   233

IT'S ALL ABOUT THE
WOMAN WHO
WEARS IT

PART I
Introduction

I associate the *it* in the title of this book, *It's All About the Woman Who Wears It*, with a woman's identity. After all, every woman wears her own unique identity in a different way. There is no wrong way to be yourself. Being a strong woman is about making the choices and decisions that come from your heart.

There are few things more powerful in the world than listening to your heart and unleashing your power to focus on what *you* want and who *you* want to be as a woman. This deep, inner realization can release a tremendous amount of strength into all areas of your life. In turn, it can affect every hat you wear in life—personal, professional, and otherwise.

I am excited about sharing my perspectives within this book with you because I *am* every woman and so are *you*. We wear many of the same hats, we conquer many of the same life challenges, we struggle with many of the same daunting questions, and at the end of the day, throughout it all, we know we can get it done. We each have that special something inside of us to overcome what often seem like insurmountable odds and make our lives work.

As women we have a certain trio of traits that allows us to succeed. Being smart, successful, and still sexy is not something we need a crash course in. Each of these qualities is woven so deeply into our innate identity as women that we could not lose them even if we tried. So I wonder what it was that tripped us up somewhere along the way. It is for this reason that I was inspired to develop my own "laws" to help us all achieve a smart, successful, and sexy identity in all areas of our lives. I knew that my task for this book would be to teach women how to tap into the strongest parts of our identities—the smartest, most successful, and sexiest pieces of ourselves—and then use that power to overcome life's most formidable obstacles.

Therefore, my own laws focus on universal issues that we have a notoriously hard time mastering on our way to success including inner strength, prioritizing our opinions over other people's opinions, living outside of our comfort zones, marriage and relationships, wasting emotions on people who just aren't worth it, friendship, balancing roles in life, pushing past fear of change and reinvention, and living with decisions once we've made them. My goal is to help us all confront these issues head-on so that we can live the best versions of ourselves as women.

As women we have more potential and power to shape our lives and the lives of those around us than most of us will ever realize. Now, all we need to do is stop getting in our own way and tap into that potential. I have written my own laws as a way of holding up a giant mirror to all of womankind and saying, Do we even realize that we are doing this, that, and whatever? Why are we doing this to ourselves?

One of the questions fans of *Cristina's Court* ask the most is whether the cases and rulings on the show are true and legally binding. In other words, viewers want to know if the show is indeed reality television.

The answer is a resounding yes! What you see is what the litigants get (although I have never personally ordered a litigant to eat bugs, like on some other reality shows). Once those bright television lights are switched off and everyone goes back to their respective corners, the litigants in *Cristina's Court* cases are legally liable to follow through with my rulings, whether they like it or not.

For the purpose of this book you are not liable or even obligated to do anything I say. Just because I call my advice *laws* does not mean my bailiff, Renard, will show up on your doorstep to enforce them. I am not a therapist, psychiatrist, or any other type of professional licensed to give you advice. But, as a lawyer and television judge, giving advice is part of my job and a responsibility that I embrace and take very seriously. Of course, my parents are not technically licensed advice givers either, yet they have always given me the best advice, hands down. Most of you would hopefully say the same thing about your own family and friends.

Think about your best girlfriend. You know the one I mean. She is the first person you call when some aspect of your life falls apart. She always gives you the best in-your-face advice that money cannot buy, and when it is time to celebrate, you know there will be a martini glass with her name on it. Even though you don't know me, and we may never have a chance to sip martinis together, I want you to think of me as that girlfriend sitting across the couch, sharing with you the best advice I can offer.

If you have seen me in action on my television shows or otherwise, you know that I am physically incapable of holding back my honest, blunt opinion about people and the situations they get themselves into. Believe me when I say this comes from a helpful place. I never judge for the sake of just judging or yell for the sake of just yelling. Judge for yourself, but the advice I give is genuine, sincere, and always from my heart.

As a way of sharing the advice in this book with you, I have gathered a collection of my observations, my personal frustrations, my experiences, my friends' experiences, and highlights of cases from *Cristina's Court*. This collection addresses the most common mistakes I see women make that sabotage us from reaching our full potential. Believe me, I have heard enough disturbing life stories from female litigants and friends in my life to know that there are things we need to know about ourselves and things we can change to eliminate an awful lot of drama and heartbreak in our lives.

These laws will teach or remind you of ways to avoid these downfalls and allow you to make the best life choices that honor who you are and empower you. The laws are held together by advice and real-life stories that I firmly believe will help women stop making the same mistakes that we have been making *forever*.

One of the common denominators in all of these stories is women trying to change who they are for someone else. I have watched them take away from their power in order to please a man, not to mention a friend, family member, colleague, or employer.

Why do we *do* this? Is it because we're still secretly buying into the old-fashioned fantasy that men don't *want* a smart, successful, sexy, empowered woman who is comfortable in her own skin and *owns* her identity? If you follow that reasoning, then yes, I suppose when a lone woman who did not get that memo breaks free from the pack and "flaunts" her strength, the rest of the pack could get really upset with her for breaking ranks.

Here is the problem with that theory: It is absolute hogwash. Men are *not* intimidated by strong women (decent men, anyway). A good man knows that a smart and strong woman does not in any way threaten his own intelligence or self-worth. A good man will admire intelligence and strength in the woman he loves. Not only that, he will find it completely sexy in every way!

Does this mean that you, as a woman, have to deny that in the deepest part of your soul you really would love to be protected and lovingly cared for by the legendary knight in shining armor? Absolutely not! It does not have to be so black-and-white. There is a term I created, largely tongue in cheek, called *confused feminism*, which means that you don't have to choose. You can be a strong, successful, smart, sexy, empowered woman who also loves to cook and clean, and take on most of the child rearing while attending to your other "traditional" responsibilities—because that is what you want. And there is nothing confusing about this. There is no wrong way to be yourself. Let me repeat that: *There is no wrong way to be yourself.* As long as you are sure that your identity is based on what you want to be and not what others wish you to be.

Another common denominator of women's behavior that I have observed is that we can be absolutely ruthless with one another. When we lose our nerve to reach for success on our own, we turn around and try to eliminate the competition instead with covert jealousy.

Women can be experts at talking one another down for being smart, sexy, and successful. When translated, those qualities can easily be perceived as a woman being a know-it-all and power hungry. We sometimes undervalue the road a woman takes to reach this level of success and empowerment. We lessen the value because it is not ours. When we see a smart, successful, sexy woman on television, or at work, or in life, our first reaction can be a little cynicism mixed with doubt. We ask ourselves how she got where she is or whom she knows and whether this woman is for real. We are afraid of gaining this powerful identity for ourselves, and the way we convey that is to degrade and put down those who have it. Is our worst weakness never looking at the value of the accomplishment?

Overlooking the accomplishments of others and trying to cut them down is not the smartest of decisions and usually leads to hurtful consequences. We could do away with most of our woman-versus-woman battles—in the workplace and, even worse, in friendship—if we could just learn to stop being jealous of one another.

Think about an empowered woman. Rather than gaining power from that woman who exhibits resourcefulness, passion for what she does, and strength of spirit, are we intimidated by her instead? We may see her as a threat to our own identity. We may be afraid that we can never be that strong, or do not deserve to be that strong, so we either shrink into a corner or, even worse, attack. I don't mean with fists and swords. When we are intimidated and jealous, what is our weapon of choice? The braver of the husbands and boyfriends will tell you in a second—our mouths! Boy, can we degrade a fellow woman when our emotions take over. Just because she has something we do not, because she has that strength just emanating from her and we do not see it in ourselves, we feel like it is our job to level her.

Even if you are protesting, yelling that this is not you, I want you to be sure of that. For example, how often do you use the phrase, "I'm jealous of . . . ," or, "I wish I . . . ," even if in your mind you are kidding? When someone else starts speaking negatively about a female friend or colleague, how often do you jump in and agree? When you hear about the successes of a strong woman, is your first reaction to be glad for her and gain inspiration to create your own success? Or does the devil with the red dress on your shoulder contemplate whom that woman may have . . . um, befriended on the way to the top? Be honest! The only way we are ever going to slay the monster is by facing it directly in the mirror.

This is not the time to be in denial or self-righteous. This is the time to get real. I am telling you this now so you are in the right frame of mind while reading the rest of the book. This is the same advice I have given to my friends, and I consider it an absolute privilege to be able to share it with you.

It seems like every time I look around, I see women taking away their personal power by continually making the same mistakes. I created these laws to remind us all how important it is to stay grounded, allowing us to make smart decisions in life.

In the context of this book I don't have the gavel power to order you to take these laws to heart. However, from one woman to another, I ask that you give each of these laws a chance. Creating, maintaining, and developing an empowered identity that incorporates all the best things about you and what you have to offer is a work in progress. If only it were as easy as mixing that martini.

But with strength comes plenty of responsibility. Accountability is a heavy hat to wear. As women, sometimes we find it hard to truly understand our roles in society simply because we wear so many hats that culminate in a job title something like this: "executive chef, chauffeur, housecleaning crew, caretaker in chief, parental referee, motivational speaker, and decorator also in charge of holding the workplace together so entire corporations don't fall apart because you called in sick one day to take your kid to the doctor." If women rested all their hats on a hat tree it would have toppled over a long time ago.

People often ask me, "Cristina, *how* do you do it?" Well, I was raised knowing that I could. I have a father who never accepted defeat. He never took no for an answer when it came to fulfilling his dream. He persevered, raised a family, and became the best professional, father, and overall human being that he could possibly be. He never sacrificed a single piece of his identity to accomplish this. He is a superb surgeon, an extraordinary father, and no words can describe his value as a human being.

One of the reasons he was able to become all this and more is because of the incredible, empowered woman at his side. My mother loves my father so much that she was never afraid to give up her own dream to support his. In a way, his dream became her new dream. She became the strength of our family, juggling more roles and responsibilities than any of us ever would have imagined at the time and making it all look seamless. I never completely understood all that my mother did, because she made it look so easy. She may have sacrificed her dream of becoming a lawyer, but she *never* sacrificed a single piece of her identity.

I am inspired by my mother's example, but never in a million years would I dream of trying to duplicate the amazing woman that she is, simply because I am not her and, in doing so, I would lose the identity that she taught me to create for myself. My wonderful, wise executive producer of *Cristina's Court*, Peter Brennan, reinforced this lesson. When the show first started, he told me, "Cristina, you need to be yourself. If you try to be anyone else, people are going to see right through you." He's right, of course.

When you try to be someone other than yourself, you are erasing and negating your own strengths, weaknesses, worth, and desire. However, when you are inspired by someone you will feel it like heat radiating from them. Inspiration opens up a new way of thinking and plants the seeds of ideas in your head. Through inspiration you will find your own strength and your own avenue for expressing it.

I am personally inspired by women whom I see struggling every day. I know they are working hard and that nothing in life comes easily for them. I see them trying to juggle their many roles and responsibilities and I can relate to that. I am inspired by them to continue being the best version of myself.

Creating and maintaining your own identity is a cycle that starts up again every time you add a new role or relationship to your life. The great thing about these laws is that you can read the book in sequence the first time. After that, hold on to it as a quick reference guide for times when your life falls out of balance and you need some specific advice for setting it right again. As women we are constantly evolving based on the roles we take on in life, how we balance them, and, most important, the lessons we learn from those experiences. We reinvent ourselves when we feel secure in our life and when we feel the time is right to take a risk. It is good practice to play with and grow within all these roles in our life.

While you are reading my own laws think about how to apply them to your own life. This has absolutely everything to do with creating your identity from the inside out. My laws may help you create that in every area of your life—work, emotions, relationships, friendship, marriage, family, and more—and then teach you how to live with the unique, empowered identity you have created.

Yes, it takes a lot of strength and effort just to accept the challenge of being a strong, successful, sexy, and smart woman. It is easy to forget how much potential we have to take on such an identity. Many women I have encountered are simply afraid because they don't know their own potential. They don't know where to start. They don't know if someone or something is waiting around the corner to take it all away. They don't know whether they will be able to become the person that secretly they know they already are. They don't realize that all they need to do is start. So let's start!

PART II
Identifying with Yourself

CHAPTER I

Law #1: *Find Strength in Yourself*

My first semester of law school was hard. All of law school was a challenge, but I had a particularly difficult time in the first semester. My grades were not reflecting my knowledge and passion for the law. I needed to find out how to sync everything up. In search of professional guidance, I met with one of the deans at my school. Trusting that she had the knowledge and resources to get me back on track and help me move forward toward my dream of becoming a lawyer, I shared all my concerns, my fears, and my questions with her. I finished my story and waited for the pearls of wisdom to start flowing from across the desk.

Without even looking at my file or asking me a single question, she suggested that perhaps law school was not for me at all. The details of this life-changing event are still so vivid in my memory almost twenty years later. I remember this woman's demeanor, the way she spoke, and how she delivered her verdict.

I felt like the rug had been ripped out from under me, and it was difficult to even catch my breath. After that, I did what so many other women do in situations like this: I took her words completely to heart and soon convinced myself that this woman *must* be right and maybe I should think of quitting law school. But then the "I" kicked in and, like lava out of a volcano, I erupted. I was furious! I thought, *How dare she tell me what I am or am not capable of? Who is she to make these assumptions about me?*

I often wonder and even try to guess why she did it and why she handled the situation the way she did. I wonder why she said these things to me without even bothering to open my file. From her point of view, as a professional in a position of authority, she may have thought she was carrying out her responsibility and simply conveying information and informing me of the risks inherent in law school. Or perhaps at one point in her life another woman treated her this way and she was paying the "favor" forward. I guess I will never know.

But what I learned was that women in positions of power should avoid handling similar situations like this. There is the potential of changing the course of someone's life in the course of one careless conversation. They can still balance their professional responsibilities with their personal opinions. But in their position, they need to be reminded of their power to inspire a young person closer to their dreams or shoot them down before they can even get started.

This nearly happened to me. Here was this woman simply giving me her quick, offhand opinion about my situation, without really even knowing anything about me, and in my mind I *made* her words the gospel. I turned her opinion, probably one of hundreds that she gave every semester, into absolute, indisputable fact. At that point in my life I was very easily influenced by what others thought of me because I thought it was right to care. What an idiot I was! But this anger I experienced reawakened me. It made me snap out of my feelings of insecurity, and allowed me to refocus on my goals and tap into my inner strength that has never left me since.

I eventually realized that without the struggle, like the one I was experiencing in law school, what is something really worth in life? As a result of that woman challenging me, I accessed the strongest parts of myself and let my passion for the law help me soar higher than ever. I think this is when I really started to tune in to the gift of being a woman. This was the beginning of my metamorphosis.

I can't help but wonder how that dean felt when I addressed the entire school at graduation as student body president. My law school experience helped me recognize that allowing other people's opinions to dictate my point of view made absolutely no sense.

Looking back, I realize how well this demonstrates many of our most common downfalls as women. I failed to speak up for myself; I assumed that someone else knew what was best for me; I forgot to find strength in who I was; and I clearly forgot to find strength in my purpose. You see, law is and always has been more than my purpose—it is my passion. I already had an undeniable feeling of knowing this (a woman's sixth sense). I let this woman *take* that passion along with my strength of identity away from me. It still makes me angry today that I let her do this to me, even if it was for just a moment. These are things that I knew about myself, yet I allowed her to create doubt. It is dangerous not to believe in yourself and trust in yourself. Because when you do, the things you want the most in your heart can slip away.

Common Downfalls

Finding strength in yourself requires an understanding of the downfalls that we women can easily fall into. Here are the behaviors I have seen in all of us that stand in the way of our potential and never lead to the positive things in life that we all deserve.

Downfall #1: Perfectionism

There are some revealing things you will find out about me and my never boring life throughout this book. One of those things is that I am a self-proclaimed perfectionist. Actually, I would classify myself as a perfectionist in recovery, because I am aware of my habit and am constantly working to use it productively.

But while I am a perfectionist in many ways, my husband, Christopher, is not. He has managed to find the balance between being satisfied with doing a good job versus turning it into a quest for perfectionism. When I think the trash needs to be taken out now, he seems to be waiting for door-to-door sanitation service. Where I see a messy living room, he sees the perfect habitat from which to watch an all-day golf marathon on television. He's not a messy or lazy guy by any means—he has just mastered the art of prioritizing and living in the moment. I think this kind of balance exists in many marriages and this perfectionist behavior is seen in many wives, simply because of our natural desire to get everything right all the time.

Being a perfectionist can also be a very good thing. Some of the smartest, most successful, empowered women I know, like myself, are self-proclaimed type A overachieving perfectionists. The reason I list this as a downfall is because I have seen too many well-intentioned women turn perfectionism into a damaging emotional quest for a level of flawlessness that does not exist. We spread ourselves too thin and allow ourselves to carry the weight of the world on our shoulders. This may be inherent in our identities as women. Now we have to find a way to use it to our advantage.

It is so easy for us to cross the line of productive perfectionism, the kind that helps us reach our goals and make our dreams come true, into the dangerous territory of paranoid, paralyzed perfectionism that leads to nothing but guilty procrastination. How can we as women be smarter, more rational, and realistic about perfectionism instead of lapsing into a state of paralysis from analysis?

Setting boundaries is an excellent way to keep your emotions from taking charge of situations, including those where you finally realize that you are competing with yourself and nobody else is in sight. Men seem to gain so much inspiration and drive from healthy competition against one another. With women, our worst enemy and grandest competitor is ourselves. When the quest for improvement turns into the quest for perfection and then spirals off into the unattainable quest for a superhuman level of infallibility that does not exist—it's time to rein it in and get real with ourselves.

Each time you take on a new challenge or role in your life, be sure to set realistic, measurable goals. When you meet those goals, give yourself a congratulatory pat on the back and move on to the next one.

Downfall #2: Failure to Speak Up

On one particular episode of *Cristina's Court*, I had a front-row seat for a dramatic story that revealed how one woman's life went from the lowest of lows to the most triumphant rebirth, all because of this woman's realization that when you speak up, you claim your identity. Her story began when she fell in love with a man and entered into a serious relationship with him. Both were young, attractive, and in love. The relationship started off normally as far as relationships are concerned. They were happy and building a life together as husband and wife. Everything seemed as it should. But then, when she got pregnant unexpectedly, things began to change for the worse. Actually, he began to change for the much worse.

When she began to gain pregnancy weight, he became demeaning, condescending, and emotionally and verbally abusive toward her. He started cheating on her, using the fact that he didn't like how she looked as a justification.

He was the poorest excuse for a human being and definitely for a parent that I have ever met. Unfortunately, his wife was too busy rationalizing his loathsome behavior to realize this. She thought that if she hung in there, was a patient, agreeable woman and didn't rock the boat, eventually everything would work itself out. She thought that since the relationship was great before it would be great again.

She never spoke up because she felt like she could not, without consequences. She started to see herself as he did and made the excuse in her mind that yes, he was right: She was fat and pregnant and his opinions were perfectly justified. And as cruel as he was to her, she kept reassuring herself in her mind that they were going to have a family and that he was just going through a hard time. She accepted the abuse, turned a blind eye to his affairs, and told herself that everything would be okay.

She told herself this right until he walked out the door, right before she had their son. She reminded herself of this again when he told her that he did not care if she was having their son or not, because he simply was not attracted to her anymore. What a shallow thought, but not surprising coming from such a shallow, cruel human being. He left her and their son, but she kept on and tried to find a way to make things work, taking on three jobs and providing for herself and their child completely, because he totally abandoned them.

That was this woman's wake-up call. I do not know if it was the power that comes with being a parent and being responsible for the life of a child or if she was just pushed so far beyond her limits, only to be abandoned right before giving birth. Whatever the reason was, she erupted inside. She was angry with herself for keeping quiet all these years. She realized that she did not deserve to be treated this way as a woman, and how *dare* this man treat his son this way!

It was at this moment that she reclaimed her life, reclaimed her identity, and became reborn and rejuvenated in the process. She decided to be a living example for her beautiful son of what a strong woman should be. She stopped buying into all these meek excuses that we often fall back on as women, such as, "He's going through a hard time," and, "I should be patient and stand by my man no matter what." Her newfound strength of identity and her choice to stand up for herself had completely liberated her!

And as a symbol of strength and validation of who she was and that no one should be treated the way she was, like a piece of garbage, she fought back—and publicly. She sued him on *Cristina's Court* to pay back all the expenses she had paid to raise their son for the past five years.

When she told her story in the courtroom that day, and shared these realizations with every one of us who was lucky to be present, her emotionally charged words generated a palpable excitement in the room. Her story was so incredibly powerful that the audience applauded and cheered, men and women alike. I think we all sympathized with her, felt for the injustice of the situation, and were proud that she spoke up. We all learned that strength of identity and the overcoming of a personal downfall are reasons to celebrate.

I often see the fear of speaking up and the failure to do so in the strongest, most empowered, most successful women I know. They are usually the first to admit that they are afraid to speak up in the face of criticism, accusation, or other uncomfortable situations. Look what happened to me in that conversation with my law school dean. I knew what I wanted, I knew I had what it took to get it, yet at the first sign of a dissenting opinion, I backed down and let someone else make me doubt myself.

Why would a self-assured woman today who has achieved power and success in all areas of her life turn into a shrinking violet when she is offended or simply has something she needs to get off her chest? Women are such contradictions in so many ways. We have come so far in terms of shattering that glass ceiling and taking ownership of so many different roles in life. Today women can be CEOs both at home and at work. Yet when someone says something that we disagree with or that offends us, we find every reason in the world to zip our lips and turn the other cheek. Or we retreat, freeze up, and later beat ourselves up about what we should have said or done in the moment.

When we refuse to stand up for ourselves and speak up, we are admitting that our point of view and our values do not matter. This is the truth, and there are consequences. As much as we can rationalize the behavior in the moment—"I don't want to create drama"; "I will be seen as argumentative"; "Why cause trouble?"; "It is not worth it"; "At least I know what I believe"—what we have really done is slapped a piece of duct tape over our mouths and censored ourselves, all while someone is taking a shot at our identities. Having an opinion does not make you a bad person. Do not underestimate your value. It makes you who you are—and that's worth way too much to stay quiet.

Downfall #3: Storing Up Anger

We've all been here, right? The results of a woman storing up anger can range from unleashing an emotional tsunami on your unsuspecting spouse to making headlines on the evening news.

It starts innocently enough. Someone does something to tick us off, but we let it slide and stay quiet. And then they do it again . . . and again . . . and again. We never say a word. We hope that at some point the person will miraculously gain the power to read our mind, interpret our glares, and analyze our facial expressions. But they do not, and our arsenal of anger grows bigger and stronger. Until finally—we snap!

By this point our anger has nothing whatsoever to do with what ticked us off in the first place. *Everything* about this person irritates us.

Now they have no idea what they did wrong, and on top of that they think we are holding them responsible for all the ills of the world.

This happened to me after an especially stressful Saturday of working from home while juggling a million other responsibilities. I was up to my eyeballs in work, and my stress level quickly reached its boiling point. All day, it felt to me as if I were having everything dumped onto my plate and my husband was not doing anything. Every time I asked him to do something, I would get a curt, "Fine," or, "Whatever." Whether that was the reality of the situation or not, that was what I was feeling. Not so ironically, Christopher's perception of his day was not much different.

We were on each other's nerves from the moment we woke up that morning. Married couples have a way of doing this to each other sometimes, merely from being around each other more than we are around anyone else. It is human nature to get on one another's nerves. And then, all of a sudden you see a big bull's-eye on your partner's forehead and decide it is an ideal place to dump all your everyday pressures and stresses, just because he happens to be standing there. This may be a survival mechanism and ultimately your partner may understand and forgive you because he feels the same way. But in the meantime, it can get pretty messy and, in our case, become sheer entertainment for everyone around.

By that evening, when Christopher and I were out to dinner with our friends, the situation was beyond boiling. Most of our friends, especially our close ones, are used to watching Christopher and me "cross-examine" each other during harmless little public tiffs. This is one of our trademarks as a married couple, and sometimes I think we might make great subjects for a reality show. Our bickering escalated quickly to the point where our friends were laughing. They could clearly relate, and the more we argued, the harder they laughed. By the time Christopher decided to turn his request for a drink refill into a federal case with the maître d', our friends were just about rolling on the floor. This was comedy to them because, as a fellow married couple who had obviously gone a few rounds using each other for "shooting practice," they understood.

You would think the drink refills would have helped both of us, but they barely took the edge off. That night I was exhibiting a typical female downfall by discarding reason and logic in favor of stubbornly hanging in there until I was somehow proven to be right. He was being typical, stubborn, macho-man, "Nuyorican" Christopher and refusing to give an inch. We bickered all the way home. When we got home, I told Christopher to sleep in the guest room and leave me alone. I couldn't figure out how this started, but at the same time I was too frustrated to figure out how to deal with him and I just wanted to go to bed alone.

Now, I have often heard the age-old marital advice "Don't go to bed angry." I have always tried to abide by that rule as much as possible. But that night, when I could not even think straight because I was so mad, I found a caveat to that old marriage rule. I learned that once in a while you *should* go to bed angry, and here's why: When you go to bed mad there is no way you will sleep well that night—no possible way. Because you obviously love your husband, no matter how much he has angered you. There is that guilt along with the constant reel of the events of the day playing back in your mind, over and over. You are tossing and turning while asking yourself, What was worth this tortured night of not sleeping?

The situational payoff comes when you wake up the next day from an awful night of sleep. You still have residual feelings from the night before—guilt, anger, upset, etc.—and it may take a moment to remember why you are feeling this way. And then you remember. Except now, with the night separating then from now, you have gained some perspective. You see that what you thought was an all-consuming, overwhelming situation the night before is really no big deal now in the light of day.

When I woke up after that night, I felt like whatever happened was now over and behind us. I could barely remember what I was upset about. How important could it have been, that a little nighttime amnesia wiped my memory clean?

I was over it, but my husband did not yet know it. He was still in a foxhole fighting the war after the peace treaty had been signed. As I walked into the kitchen, he was huffing and puffing and stomping around, clearly without having experienced the benefits of overnight amnesia. I cheerfully offered to make him coffee. This "sudden" turn of events (in his mind) completely stumped him. He was ready for a battle and instead all he got was a cup o' joe. He was left wondering where his sparring partner had disappeared to overnight. Finally, Christopher realized that the battle was over, crawled out of his foxhole, and gave himself permission to move on.

The moral of this story is that there are many things that should be bottled up, and anger is definitely not one of them. We may think that we are being wise and tolerant, and avoiding confrontation, but somewhere inside, there is a piece of ourselves that is not ready to let go of the issue. We need to let people know if they have done something to offend or anger us. Believe me, they would rather know about it when it happens than wait for the big bang. Storing up anger does more to worsen the problem than to solve it. When we bottle up our anger now, someone always pays later.

Downfall #4: Being Passive-Aggressive

Passive-aggressive behavior is, according to the Mayo Clinic Web site: "A pattern of expressing your negative feelings in an indirect way—instead of openly addressing them." This is not healthy for the soul.

The passive-aggressive personality gene is not implanted only in women. In fact, none of these downfalls are uniquely attributable to women. However, in my experience we women seem to fall prey to these behaviors most often.

If the world were ruled exclusively by passive-aggressive personalities we would be done for. Yet there are women who actually believe that being passive-aggressive gets them what they want. They believe that it is a crafty way to make a point, teach someone a lesson, or get back at someone.

I remember a case on *Cristina's Court* that is a violent, real-life example of passive-aggressive behavior. Three young women found themselves involved in a love triangle. When one girl found out that her girlfriend had another girlfriend, she decided to get even. Rather than confronting either one, the girl decided to enact her revenge, driven by feelings of rage, on the car windshield belonging to her ex-girlfriend.

Yes, this is an extreme version of how a typical passive-aggressive situation plays out. But it made me think twice about what was going on. I asked myself, *What kind of emotions are in her head that would make her do something so violent?* It is still debilitating to me as a human being to think that such overwhelming, irrational emotion can happen to anybody if we fail to control ourselves and see the bigger picture.

The defendant in my courtroom during the case actually admitted that she really just wanted to hit her girlfriend. But she took it out on the car instead as a relatively safe adversary. And we had the chilling videotape to prove exactly how violently this delicate-looking young woman took out her aggressions on the car. Surveillance cameras captured the scene as she exited the store into the parking lot, seemingly calm, except carrying a baseball bat at her side. In the courtroom we all watched the surveillance video in disbelief as it showed her raising the baseball bat high over her head. In one tremendous blow after another, this petite woman shattered the windshield of the car.

When the video ended, there was silence in the courtroom. Everyone in the room was dumbfounded by what we had just seen; everyone except the defendant herself. She stood there, head held high, smiling and looking as proud as an Oscar nominee who had just watched a clip from her nominated film.

I looked the defendant in the eyes and asked her, "Do you feel good now?" She smiled as if to say yes. I looked at her again and said, "How embarrassing." The tough-girl facade suddenly melted. She looked back at me with tears in her eyes and an expression of shame on her face. I felt for her because I felt shame too. Here was this bright, beautiful woman who did a really stupid thing that stole her strength and identity as a woman.

This type of avoidance behavior is becoming more prevalent as people become more and more fearful of confronting their problems. But there are always going to be circumstances in the world that seep over into our lives. Sometimes it just seems easier to hide than to confront our problems. Because when we face what has gone wrong in our lives, it is inevitable to start questioning whether we did something to cause it. I have found that the people who choose to hide rather than stand up, take their punches, and learn their lessons are the ones most prone to manipulating their way out of dicey situations instead of dealing with them.

It's okay to be scared, anxious, and emotionally exhausted at times. We have all been there. There are many healthy ways of dealing with those times. What is unhealthy is using the bad times in your life as an excuse to dump on other people.

How could we have so little regard for another human being that it would be easier to take something out on them rather than directly confronting them and solving the problem at hand? It takes a lot more energy to be covert and sneaky than it does to be open and honest.

Downfall #5: Making Assumptions

As Felix Unger from *The Odd Couple* once said in one of that show's famous episodes, "When you assume you make an 'ass' out of 'u' and 'me.'" We have all heard it over and over, but how well do we take it to heart? There is an immense amount of truth in this saying, yet I see us all continue to get ourselves into repeated sticky situations because of an assumption we have made about a particular person or a incident.

Someone once said that it is a woman's prerogative to change her mind. This is not bad, and it definitely keeps things exciting (although I'm not sure my husband would always agree). Because if we were predictable, open books who never changed our minds, assumptions would be fine. When we make assumptions we are pretending the world is predictable. We are saying, "Just because you walk around upright on two legs like me, it is safe to assume that you would do and think the exact same thing in this situation that I would." What an insult to someone's unique identity. Assuming is a waste of time, and it almost always leads to confusion and complications.

Downfall #6: Overreacting

All I have to do is bring up the subject of when women overreact with my husband and the responses I get from him range from eyes rolling into the back of his head to, "Watch out," to the "I'm not going there" hands-up-in-the-air gesture similar to something you might see a person do on *When Animals Attack!*

When we overreact to something someone else says or does, we are not making the valid point we think we're making. We are not teaching anyone a lesson, because it's likely they have no idea what set us off in the first place. Whatever we think we are accomplishing by overreacting, we are not.

People do not respond nearly as well to an over-the-top show of emotion or a temper tantrum as they do if we speak quietly, *purposefully*, and make our point. Speaking softly to get our point across demonstrates an incredible inner strength and self-confidence that opens many more doors to success in all areas of life than screaming our way through at an emotional fever pitch.

Downfall #7: I'm Just Kidding

I'm not kidding, actually. Having a sense of humor is great. Being the joke-telling center of attention is awesome and also very sexy in the smart woman who can pull it off. What I am referring to with those three little words is the reverse disclaimer that women often tack onto the end of potentially harmful sentences. This also falls into the passive-aggressive category at times.

For instance, a woman really wants to say something that might not be the kindest thing in the world to say to or about someone. She just cannot hold it back. But she knows it will tarnish the image she has worked so hard to create of a good woman who would never let an unkind word slide from her lips. What to do? Tack on the "I'm just kidding" disclaimer at the end of the comment and all will be forgiven. An insult is an insult, no matter how you frame it or disclaim it.

Another kind of "I'm just kidding" is the self-deprecating kind, a direct shot at yourself with nobody to run interference. "I'm so fat I don't know how any man could love me—just kidding." How can you find strength in your own identity if you are always taking masked shots at it? Please don't misunderstand me—I have nothing against making jokes. I love to laugh more than most people. We all just need to make sure that if we are going to make a joke, it is not at the expense of our precious selves or others.

Downfall #8: Making Accusations

Have you ever been so wrapped up in the heated emotions of a moment, where you feel betrayed or wronged in some way, and are about to pull the trigger and let a very harsh accusation fly? I know I have. This is a tricky one for women, because once someone or something puts us on the defensive—watch out!

There is nothing wrong with standing up for yourself or your loved ones and refusing to let someone take a stab at your integrity. The way in which you handle the situation, however, can make or break relationships. Speaking up is a good thing, but being aware of how we do it in the heat of the moment is even better. When someone pushes our buttons our first reaction is to say what we feel we need to say, using the first uncensored words that come to mind. It is like we have a load of poison on our chests that we just want to dump on someone else— right now! We make irrational accusations and jump the gun a lot more quickly than men, because we are more emotional by nature then men. Again, there are ways of using our emotion and passion to our advantage. This is not one of them.

Our instinct to accuse first and ask questions later is why e-mail drafts exist, as well as pens and paper. Get it off your chest—type it, write it, or say it into a tape recorder. Pretend you are writing or saying what you actually would say. Now take a deep breath and look at what you have written with a rational, discerning eye. Would you want someone to say that to you? Think about how it will help you reach your purpose. There is always a better way to still get your point across without the poison. I suspect that many business and personal relationships have been saved simply by people taking a breath and doing a rewrite.

Downfall #9: Not Saying What We Mean

She: Well, what did you *think* I meant?

He: I thought you meant what you said!

She: How could you think that? Don't you even *know* me?

Yes, of course he knew what she meant, because he's a mind reader. All men are, right? It is high time that we stop speaking in the coded, masked subtleties that can be understood only by CIA agents and lead people to wonder if even *we* know what we mean.

Clear communication is an amazing gift and a very powerful tool of the smart, successful woman. Do not complicate things on purpose. When we remove the mind and word games and just say what we mean, our lives will be much less complicated. I firmly believe that when we say our life is too complicated it's usually because *our own* actions are complicating it.

Here is a refreshing example from *Cristina's Court* of a woman who is the exact opposite. This particular litigant leads a life that is strangely straightforward and uncomplicated because she says exactly what she means. Life is simple for her. The problem was that the defendant in the case was the exact opposite. Perhaps he had too much past experience with women who play games and he was confused by a straightforward woman like this. Regardless of the reason, during the course of this case this woman managed to enlighten him.

It all started when the plaintiff in the case, the woman, advertised online for a bicycling friend. That was literally all she wanted—a friend to bicycle with. She wanted friends with no benefits and she meant it. She thought she had found one in a man who responded to her ad. The problem was that he decided to read into the subtext of the ad and put the moves on his new bicycle friend. But there *was* no subtext in the ad. At least, the plaintiff did not think so.

She was honestly surprised by this man's advances and clearly confused by how this had happened. I believed this, because everything about this woman was direct and straight to the point.

The more stereotypical version of this story would have the roles reversed, and the woman reading too much into something that was not there. There are certainly enough stories floating around about women who mistake a friendly smile for a marriage proposal. This woman, on the other hand, lives an uncomplicated existence that became needlessly complicated by the arrival of this bicycle friend who thought they were more than friends. Everything came to a head when he finally borrowed money from her. He was certain that he was in a relationship that was going somewhere. She was certain that her bicycle buddy would pay back the borrowed money at some point, because that is the reasonable thing to do. Big mistake!

Well, obviously, had he returned the loan I never would have had the pleasure of meeting this bicycling noncouple. I set things right according to the letter of the law, but what I learned from the case was about much more than returning a loan. When you say what you mean and mean what you say, and believe that everyone else is doing the same, life has a way of being much less complicated.

So there you have it—the top nine downfalls that trip us up the most on the road to reaching our smart, successful, and sexy potential. These may be downfalls but they do *not* have to be detours. Once we recognize the weakest parts of our identity, we are ready to power forward and discover the strength within.

Finding Strength in Your Identity

There is a popular old song that goes: "You've got to accentuate the positive / Eliminate the negative / Latch on to the affirmative / Don't mess with Mister In-Between." Now that we have recognized our downfalls and weaknesses, it is time to focus on our strengths. Let's learn to accentuate our positives!

Finding strength in yourself means finding strength in your own identity, your actions, and your own uniqueness. These are the things that make you strong, and what make you different from the next woman. There is nothing wrong with the next woman; but she is not you.

What do you like about yourself? What do you need to let go? Look to the women you trust and admire as inspiration without feeling like it is a contest to see who is the better woman.

I have been blessed with many women whom I trust and admire and look to for inspiration. One of those women, my mentor throughout my career, also happens to be one of the top lawyers in the nation in her field. Many people are intimidated by this woman, especially those who do not know her well and judge the book by its cover. Because this woman's "cover" is very guarded, beautiful, reserved, and extremely professional. When you are as highly regarded and accomplished in your profession as she is, it is not unusual to keep your guard up and hesitate before letting people in and trusting them. This is because people can often be so judgmental, particularly of those who have achieved such a high level of success. This is especially true around newcomers who never take the chance to get to know her. These are the very people who have the most negative first impression of her. You can see how it's a vicious cycle.

But I see it a little differently than they do. When I look at this woman, my mentor and friend, I see an incredibly smart businesswoman with *unbelievable* strength and uniqueness of identity. I did from the first moment I met her. She inspires me to nurture my own strength of identity.

As my friend, she teaches me to take pride in who I am without ever making excuses or apologies for it. Boy, would the people intimidated by this woman be surprised if they knew the woman I know—a genuinely warm, fun, down-to-earth woman (who also loves to let her hair down and have fun). She is also the proud mother of a son who graduated from a top military school.

As my mentor, she has always taken me under her wing and taught me career lessons that helped shape my roles as a professional woman, business owner, and lawyer. I have learned so much from her. She is such a great example of how valuable a mentor can be in life, personally and professionally. Whom you choose as a mentor reflects who you are as a person and who you are working to be.

I personally look up to women like my friend who manage to balance many personal and professional roles in life and still find time to give back to the community. It takes time, effort, and commitment to do this. So when individuals who have many demands placed on them invest the time necessary to inspire, help, and guide another person, it is truly noteworthy. It would obviously be much easier for her to keep her head down and be conscious only of her own life. Instead, she chooses to stay true to her own identity while being conscious of others around her (like myself) who would love nothing more than to gain an ounce of her knowledge and experience.

An important aspect of a woman with a complete identity is knowing what she wants but never forgetting that others around her might not have the certainty and may be looking for inspiration. She is generous with her time and knowledge, never fearing that if she shares this piece of herself, her protégé will overtake her professionally. There is no room for jealousy in mentorship, only a genuine desire to give of oneself.

Nonetheless, as generous and genuine as I find this woman to be, I have watched people continue to make negative assumptions about her, and learned that first impressions and snap judgments are an unavoidable part of life. But when we judge a book by its cover, as so many people do of her, we miss out on an opportunity to connect with and become inspired by truly remarkable people. In my case, I would have missed out on a mentor, an inspiration, and a cherished friend.

As life would have it, I have another sexy, smart, successful girlfriend who is judged based on the sexy first and the smart second, a lot more often than she would prefer. And referring to her simply as sexy and smart would be seriously selling this woman short. She is by far one of the classiest, most selfless, doting, nurturing, intelligent, successful professional women I—and most people who meet her—have ever encountered. She is the very definition of some of the best things about a woman. She naturally puts everyone else's needs in front of her own. These selfless qualities, combined with her innate feminine beauty, are qualities that I admire in her and, in the spirit of judging a book by its cover, these are the things that most other people also see first and admire about her.

I know that my friend struggles with this. It is not that she does not value these parts of her identity. She exudes self-confidence and security about every aspect of herself. Her struggle often comes from balancing these qualities with professional success she has fought hard for and earned as a television producer. I can attest from firsthand experience that she is an extremely intelligent producer with an incredible eye for television and choosing the stories that work in that medium. She also happens to be married to one of the most powerful individuals working in the industry. In her own right, she has the strength of identity, smarts, and savvy to work side by side with her husband.

The frustration for my friend comes when people either do not see the value of her individual professional identity, they simply see her as an extension of her powerful husband, or they see her physical beauty first and her professional accomplishments second. This quickly changes as soon as they deal with her professionally and realize that she is brilliant. In many ways, her natural urge to nurture combined with her incredible career success make her Mrs. Cleaver, accidentally stuck in 2009.

I look up to my friend because of her amazing, complete, and secure identity. I have seen in her that even when she gets occasionally frustrated by her own contradictions, she never takes her identity for granted. She wears every aspect of it with pride, grace, and always generosity. I admire her as someone who has it all and sometimes does not even realize it.

Now it's your turn. I want you to picture in your mind's eye a woman in your life who inspires you to strengthen your own unique identity, whether she is your mother, sister, grandmother, aunt, best friend, mentor, or another woman you admire.

What traits, good or bad, does she have that you do not? What strengths and characteristics does she possess that you do not, and vice versa? When you compare, you can gain inspiration from someone's strengths. I know it's tough for some of us to compare ourselves to one another without considering it competitive or unkind, or risking someone taking something the wrong way. But it does not have to be this way. All you are doing is using someone close to you as inspiration to create a wish list for designing your own unique identity.

In order to create your own identity and then find strength within it, focus on the thing you are most passionate about, the thing that radiates into every single area of your life. For me, that thing is the law. What is your own starting point—your driving force? I realize it is a popular notion to encourage people to start fresh with a blank slate at the beginning of any improvement process. I personally disagree with this idea.

After all, when someone is a blank slate, anyone can write on them. If you are creating a powerful, unique personal identity, then why on earth would you want to turn the process into an act of Congress, where anyone who comes along with an opinion about you has the power to determine who *you* are? This may be why so many of us are confused about who we are. As women, we seem to have some twisted implant hidden deep within our human nature that makes us constantly seek validation and approval for every decision we make, from what cereal to have for breakfast to whom we should marry and what we should do for a living. Again, we underestimate our worth. Your identity belongs to you. There is no other identity like it, and nobody has the right to write on it without your express permission.

My strong feelings on the subject of identity and self-confidence were instilled in me by my parents. They have always been two incredibly strong individuals whose entire life stories have been defined by strength of character, self-reliance, and resilience in the face of adversity and life challenges. My parents taught me that no matter what life throws at you, know that you can always count on *yourself.* Obviously, I know I can count on my husband, my siblings, my mother and father, and my friends—they are all selfless people, and I am blessed to have them in my life. Look around you and I'm sure you can say the same thing about the people in your life. But there is nothing better than knowing you can always count on yourself under the best and worst of circumstances.

The support of my loved ones in no way contradicts the knowledge that I can count on myself for everything I want and need in life. It is so easy to forget that your biggest personal strength is being able to count on yourself. You know in your heart that when it comes right down to it, you are always going to be there for yourself. It takes some time, along with maturity and age, to fully arrive at this realization, but once you get there it is truly a great feeling knowing you can depend on yourself. You truly are the master of your domain, and that knowledge is the foundation of an empowered identity.

Finding Strength in Your Own Opinion

As women, self-doubt can be our biggest weakness. Now add another layer of insecurity that comes when we allow other people's opinions of us to multiply that self-doubt. It is amazing how we are constantly looking outside of ourselves for some magical secret to life when we already have everything we need, usually untapped, within us. However, when we do not get the magic beans from those around us, we are tempted to settle instead for an unhealthy dose of judgment and opinions in their place.

Why do we really care so much what other people think of us and of the decisions we make? They are not living our lives. They are not going to take responsibility for our choices, successes, and failures. As my husband frequently asks me, "Why do you care what they think of you?"

This is an excellent question that many people have tried to answer. In fact, an entire industry has sprung up in an attempt to answer the questions of why we care so much about the opinions of others, why we are always seeking reassurance, and how to put a stop to it.

The business of self-help, which, as many other people have pointed out, is a complete oxymoron, started gaining momentum in the early 1990s with the popularity of personal mentors. I find this interesting because, as you read earlier, my perspective on mentors is a very positive one and refers to one person providing guidance for another and sharing their expertise, usually in the context of a career.

In contrast, the kind of mentorship trend I am referring to is the kind of personal life coaching that the popular television series *Seinfeld* immortalized in one of its episodes. In the episode, there was a female character (not Elaine) Jerry Seinfeld was dating, who apparently could do little more than get out of bed in the morning without checking in with her mentor for validation and reassurance that yes, indeed, getting out of bed in the morning is a positive life step. This woman was literally paralyzed in her own fear and indecisiveness about how to live her life. Finally, the mentor moved on, presumably to better-paying customers, and Jerry's girlfriend was left helpless, squealing, "What will I do without a mentor? Who will tell me what to do?" Jerry immediately responded, to a round of laughter from the studio audience, "I can be your mentor. I can tell you what to do!" The lesson is that someone is always around who is perfectly willing to tell you what to do. Whether what they're telling you makes any sense for your life and is in any way healthy for you is highly debatable. Remember that next time you look around without any discretion for the first opinion that comes your way. It may sound good, but ask yourself what they know that you don't about yourself.

Well, the mentoring movement soon gave way to the life-coaching industry. Now it seems every time I look around there is a new life coach, transformation guide, or inspirational leader offering to give us the answers that we are apparently incapable of finding for ourselves—for a nominal fee, of course. Do we have such a lack of confidence in our own lives that we need to go outside of ourselves to have them fixed? How sad is that!

The hidden message conveyed to anyone who chooses to pay money for life coaching seems to be this: The advice I am giving you about your life had better change something or you have spent a pretty penny for nothing. Here is this life coach dissecting your life, and telling you who they have decided you are, making judgments about your life and telling you how to fix it, when you already have these answers embedded deep within your identity.

I am not "broken" and neither are you. We are all imperfect human beings living imperfect lives and we are going to make mistakes. No amount of self-confidence, mystical power of intention, self-awareness, and personal development "tools" will prevent us from making mistakes. We are going to make mistakes and that is reality.

This does not mean that we need to find an outside solution to our problems. We have the power to fix our problems ourselves by addressing them when we first come across them. Isn't recognizing our own faults the best form of therapy? There is also so much to be gained when we are accountable and take responsibility for our mistakes as well as our triumphs.

I was once watching a prime-time television show where a father's son was tragically killed. Desperate for some kind of "closure" because of the overwhelming guilt he felt, having never told his son that he loved him, the father sought out the services of a psychic to communicate with the spirit of his dead child. Well, the psychic phone lines must have been jammed that day, because the psychic couldn't make a connection with the son. The part of the show that had me applauding from my couch was when the psychic got real with the father. He told the dad, "Listen, you shouldn't be looking to me or anybody else to get closure or whatever it is you're looking for with your son. You should have told your son when he was alive that you loved him instead of hiring some stranger to take over that responsibility as his father."

Yet as women we do this every day! We are looking for closure, validation, and everything else in the world that we have the power to give ourselves, from everyone in the world except ourselves.

This still doesn't answer the question of why we are like this, especially as women, in the first place. Here is my best explanation: The idea of women feeling the need to look outside of ourselves for answers is directly connected to our history. Women have historically held a more "secondary" role to men in terms of men being the patriarchal breadwinners, heads of the family, and such. Yes, that has obviously changed in the past few decades, but if we deny how we started, we are denying information that we can all learn from.

Men are more secure in themselves because they have always had a very secure role in society. Their roles have been pretty clearly defined for a long time, and therefore they've had little reason to doubt themselves. Would you ever hear a man referred to as "just a . . ." anything, like women are often referred to as "just a housewife" or "just a stay-at-home mom"? I seriously doubt it. Men's roles in society have had a long time to become cemented, and all the hats they wear are firmly planted on their heads.

We women, on the other hand, are a constantly and rapidly evolving work in progress. Look at how much our roles have changed and how society's perceptions of us have changed in such a relatively short period of time. With the feminist movement, we have put up our dukes and tried to fight our way from a secondary to a primary role. We felt so offended that we were viewed as secondary in any way that we felt like we had to come out running.

Don't get me wrong; as women we have had ample inner strength to get the job done. However, also as women we cannot deny our emotions, and our natural tendency to analyze and overanalyze life, something that probably started as a valuable survival skill. At the heart of it all we are sensitive souls with an acute awareness of what we are feeling without always knowing why we are feeling it.

This has led to an internal battle that most of us are not even aware we're fighting. On one hand, we have gained so much in the fight to prove that we are as worthy of a primary role in life as men are. On the other hand, there are all of the aggressive emotions that have emerged as by-products of that battle. "Look at my accomplishments! I'm just as good as you are and I will prove it, prove it some more, and prove it again and again until I think you are hearing me!"

It is to the point where I wonder whom we are proving our worth to. There is certainly a part of society that will not always see a woman's full worth. I cannot do anything about that and neither can you, so let's stop banging our heads against the wall. How much do we need to continue overreacting and overcompensating before we realize that most people really do measure your worth by your actions, accomplishments, and who you are, and not by gender?

But "they" are not really thinking about you much at all, especially your fellow women, who may possibly be too busy thinking the same things about you. It is funny: We are all walking around with this paranoia that everyone is so obsessed with us, observing us twenty-four hours a day like lab rats, and making personal and harsh judgments about every choice we make, when in reality people couldn't care less. I am not saying that people couldn't care less about your existence and well-being, especially your loved ones. I am saying that they are not obsessing over you in the way that you think they are based on the fantasy you have created in your mind. Did I mention that one of a woman's greatest strengths and weaknesses is her imagination? It is so much better when we harness our imaginations for good instead of evil!

As we continue battling these invisible forces externally, the struggle has also become an internal one. The more we struggle externally with the challenges in our lives, the more we think we need to rage against the machine inside. This has turned into a widespread phenomenon of insecurity in many of us. We climbed the mountain so fast, without stopping to see how far we'd come and admire the view, that suddenly we arrived at the top. We then looked down—and believe me, it's a long way down, because we have come that far—and became terrified. It is our natural urge to question everything, as women, so the questions started flying, fast and furious. "Do I deserve to be here?" "Did I earn this?" "What will people think of my achievement?"

We are so preoccupied with this eternal, constant vying for public approval that it frequently becomes an obsession. How many times have you left a conversation, started playing it back in your mind, berated yourself based on how you handled it, and then rewritten a new script in your mind about how you wish you had handled it?

This especially happens when we are trying to make a good first impression. That's when we really turn the out-of-control imagination machine into high gear. Taking it a step further, do you then start trying to guess what the other person is thinking of you now? This really has to be the best soap opera in the world we have created. We are now projecting dialogue into another person's head about what they think of us, and they have no idea we are doing it. If you actually told them what you were thinking, I guarantee you would get a baffled look in return. Especially considering that they projected the same type of script onto you. With all this made-up drama and inventing of problems that do not exist, it is really amazing that we can get anything done in life. With all the hats we have to wear as women, it's time we take off the one that makes us obsessed with what other people may or may not think of us.

Here is something else I find completely contradictory and always interesting: Children do not seem to have this problem. Why don't they care what people think? We do not think of them as mature enough to have developed an identity, self-worth, and a secure impression of who they are. Yet they certainly act like they have those things cemented sometimes. For example, think about what happens when one child says to another, "You're funny-looking!" and the recipient simply knows it is not true. The recipient responds in an instant: "No, I'm not!" and they move on and continue playing. I have learned from my daughter that kids know an awful lot more about themselves and how the world works than we think they do.

Maybe we start with evolved identities and a sense of who we are. Then, as we get older, we start questioning ourselves, because that is what society tells us we are supposed to do or be. We start questioning everything about ourselves, and then other people, and then eventually it comes full circle to what other people think of us. Do we already have a unique, completely formed, healthy identity as children and then allow it to fall apart in the face of adversity as we get older? We need to look to children, younger versions of ourselves, as a reminder that the only person you really have to please in life is yourself.

It is okay, of course, to have a *healthy* awareness of how you are being perceived. This is the same self-protection mechanism that keeps us from leaving the house in the morning without pants on. However, it is important to select which opinions matter the most to you, which ones are most productive to your life, and which opinions truly honor and respect your identity. If you accept all the garbage without any kind of filter, what kind of identity are you building for yourself? You are creating a weak one that is a poor reflection of who you really are. Make sure that if you choose to accept someone else's opinion of you as fact (emphasis on the word *choose*), you are sure that person has your best interests in mind and respects who you are, not who they want you to be.

What is the solution? How do we fight our very instincts as women to seek the validation and approval that we feel can come only from others? I have to take a reality check and look at myself in the mirror. I have to find the inner strength to ask myself, *What really matters most to me?* The best time to do this for me is when I am alone. When I'm alone I realize what is really important to me, without being influenced by the constant current of public opinion. I realize it's the very basic things in life that are important: being with people who make me happy, being with people who make me feel absolutely myself and complete, and being with the people who bring me the most happiness without having to force it.

My husband, who is also my best friend, is a great alert system who sounds whenever I start losing myself in the opinions of others. When he sees that I'm doing or saying something that does not seem to be "me," he says, "What's going on with you? What are you doing?" This usually happens when I go into a situation with a solid opinion about my point of view. He knows that my opinion is solid and so do I. Then all of a sudden I come back with a different opinion of what I was supposed to do in the situation, and now I am acting wishy-washy. The alert sounds for both of us because I started doubting myself and became like somebody else.

When I find strength in my own opinion, there is no chance of that kind of situation happening. There is no doubt in my mind that I am being true to myself and acting on my own opinions and intentions.

Finding Strength Through Purpose

Having some kind of purpose in life, no matter how well-defined or ambitious it is (I'm not suggesting that everyone should climb Mount Everest), single-handedly carves out an extremely personal and powerful part of your identity. Establishing a purpose for your very existence and the goals to achieve it is something that you carry with you every day, and that makes you unique among every other person on the planet.

No other woman could be the mother of your children, your husband's wife, your parents' daughter, or the person who follows her dreams, personal and professional, quite the way you do it. Your unique identity is shaped by your intentions, goals, triumphs, dreams, failures, pit stops, setbacks, revelations, choices, and all the people and experiences you encounter along the way.

Without some sort of purpose—a general intention of how we want our lives to look—it is easy for others to shape us with their own beliefs and opinions. We then become chameleons to transform according to whatever everyone else is projecting onto us. When people make us into what they want us to be (for their own purposes), what kind of things do you think they're projecting onto us? I will bet we are not getting their best qualities. We are getting their baggage.

Having a clear understanding of who you are, why you are here, and what you are capable of achieving in your life is the best way to keep from "blending in" and losing your sense of self.

We are all women who wear many hats, have many demands placed on us, constantly take on new responsibilities, and often wonder how we will just survive and get it all done, let alone who we are and what our purpose is. It is easier than we may think to gain strength through all those roles in our lives.

If you love doing something, it will just come naturally. Have faith in the fact that you can do it, and do it well, and your passion for what you are doing will carry you through doing it. We each have so much to offer—more than we think we do sometimes. Once we realize this, it gets easier to see our talents and life roles as valuable sources of inner strength. Then we start to see that all our responsibilities in life are really privileges.

Finding Strength in What You Already Know

The funny thing is that as women, we already *know* all of this. We know how to find strength from within. I am not reinventing the wheel here by telling you that you are a smart, successful, sexy woman with all the potential in the world to achieve whatever you want in life, including happiness. You already know you have all the potential in the world. I am just playing the part of the messenger and reminding you while also reminding myself.

As women we know a lot of things instinctively in our guts simply because we are women. I am convinced that women, for some reason, have an entirely different type of radar for life in general than men do. My husband is always the one telling me that I have the craziest intuition for things. He says that if we could bottle it and sell it we would be millionaires. I have a sixth sense about life. I feel that certain events in my life will happen and then they do. It is an indescribable feeling of knowing. This is a gift that all women have. Why do you think they call it *women's* intuition? We have this amazing gift, yet for reasons I will never understand, we don't always listen to it. When we do listen we don't believe in it, and we almost never act on it. We're all sitting on an untapped gold mine here!

Every one of you reading this knows exactly the feeling I'm talking about. It is that one hundred percent knowing of what is going to happen before it happens. Yes, doubting yourself sometimes is a healthy way to avoid stepping into something you don't want to step into. But please do not get stuck in a pile of self-doubt. Finding strength in our intuition is a powerful part of who we are as women.

Intuition is such a natural, internal thing. It goes back to our core and having the confidence to believe that we know what we know. Yet, as women in particular, we are creatures who want to constantly feel assured and validated, and be patted on the back all the time. The desire for constant reassurance is inherent in our nature. It's as if our life is a public event driven by ratings and surveys where we have to check with the pollsters before leaving the driveway every morning. This is not a presidential election; it is our life!

If you need proof, ask yourself this: How many times, when you are asking someone for an opinion about how you look, about what you're wearing, the quality of your work, or the rightness of one of your decisions, are you *actually* asking them what you say you're asking? Most of the time, aren't you really saying to them, "Please tell me I look good, I can do no wrong in my career, I am the toast of my peers, and every decision I make about anything is spot-on." The subtext of most questions we ask is, "What do you think I should do?" Listen to your heart and "know what you know," and you will realize that you know the answer to that question and all the other ones like it.

So not only can we count on ourselves, but we also can trust and believe in ourselves. If we do not trust ourselves we will have trouble trusting others as well. Suddenly we will be questioning everything and everybody in our lives. This is not a foundation for living a fulfilling life.

Here is something else that we already know as women but may need to be reminded of: We are all blessed. No matter where we come from, how much money we have, what kind of house we live in or other material possessions we have, whether we are single, married, have kids or not, whether we have a thousand family members and friends or just a small handful of loved ones—we are surrounded by good things in our lives. Sometimes we cry when we should be counting our blessings. Call them blessings, good things, gifts, or whatever words you choose, but the people and circumstances of your life belong to you, and it is important to be thankful for every one of them. These are your unique sources of strength, because they are directly attached to who you are and everything about you.

My husband, daughter, parents, family, friends, and the life I live are all incredible sources of strength and inspiration for me. Sometimes it is hard for me to truly see this until I come across others who are less fortunate in their lives. For instance, in my line of work, I am faced with a wide variety of details and circumstances from other people's lives. I have witnessed and provided guidance and resolution for situations resulting from bad choices that could have easily been pre-vented, tragic errors in judgment, and virtually every other type of human drama in between.

I heard about one of the most tragic errors of judgment I have ever seen from my bench on *Cristina's Court*. This is the story of a young mother with three children from three different fathers. The young mother was the defendant on the show, who had previously sued the "father" of one of her children for back child support. Before you ap-plaud the nobility of this mother, using a court system specifically designed to protect against parents who are truly deadbeats, pay close attention to the real story behind this case.

This man she had sued prior to coming to *Cristina's Court* was the farthest thing from a deadbeat dad that exists. He was a young, dis-abled war veteran who was never given the opportunity to raise and get to know this child, this boy that the young mother swore up and down belonged to him. The defendant had told him that he had a son, but allowed only a limited relationship between father and son. He would ask to see the child, but there was always an excuse as to why he could not. The father gradually started to suspect that perhaps the child was not his after all. In the meantime, this woman allowed her son to be-lieve that this man was his biological father. The man became even more insistent, frequently asking to see his son. It was not until he started asking repeatedly and was denied the opportunity to see his child entirely that he demanded a DNA test. He was not requesting the test to evade his responsibilities as a father to this child. What he wanted was a chance to have a relationship with his child—a relation-ship that she denied him. When he requested the DNA test, the mother cut off all communication with him and sued him for child support.

She did not just sue him either. She took him for everything he had and then some. She sued for all past child support, and won a large settlement. He could no longer support his wife and family on his dis-ability checks. His credit was ruined to the point where he and his wife were denied a government housing loan for veterans. Forget about a home loan—he could not even get cell phone service. This man was never allowed to see the boy he thought was his son, and now he was about to become bankrupt. In the end, this honorable man, this disabled veteran who was suffering through all of this in order to do the right thing, was not even the boy's biological father. What was even more appalling was that the mother knew this all along (the man and his wife had also suspected it for some time).

This was a story entirely concocted by the young mother because, in her mind, she was entitled to take this man's money. As she admitted in court, she thought he was more likely to pay than the real biological father. This sense of entitlement was insulting, and absolutely tragic for this man and his family. She was abusing the law and hurting innocent people in the process.

Here, between the lines of this case about a mother who wanted the world to know how life had wronged her and what she felt she deserved in return for her suffering, is what is so amazing about *all* the cases that came on *Cristina's Court.*

Court television may be the ultimate form of reality television and unscripted drama, with stories driven by the passion of the participants. But I have learned from the people who come on the show that this is not about claiming their fifteen minutes of fame, and it is not about the money. It is really about public validation or public vindication. The people who come on the show want their story to become public for a very specific reason.

In this case, the mother was not the only one who wanted the world to know about her hardships. The wife of the veteran was also at her wit's end with this woman, and, out of desperation, she sued the mother for emotional distress. She felt so indignant that this woman would be so careless as to abuse the law, ruin a good man's name, and affect the welfare of their family. It angered her how this woman could ruin all these lives—hers, her husband's, and their kids'—by doing something so selfish. This was her emotional outcry, to show the world that you cannot do what this mother did—to any human being— because it is wrong. And that was why they came to *Cristina's Court*.

When I delivered my verdict, I felt I had to be brutally honest with the defendant—as a judge, as a fellow mother, and as a human being. How dare she do this to her own child, making him think this man was his father when she knew that was not the case? Who gave her the right to manipulate her child's life this way? I felt strongly that I had to protect the rights of mothers who use the law correctly and need that law to protect themselves and their children while also protecting unfairly framed men like the plaintiff.

My instinct for fairness was insulted by the audacity of this self-centered woman who reeked of the entitlement that is an epidemic in today's world. She felt that because *her* life was so difficult and because *she* was supporting three kids, she was entitled to whatever she could get in life. She had become the master of a truly psychotic game and left nothing but devastation and hardship in her wake.

Long after I set things right from a legal standpoint, awarding this man the maximum financial reward allowed, this story stayed with me. Actually, it still stays with me to this day.

What also stayed with me about this case was the strength, grace, and resilience of that man's wife. I looked at her and saw the epitome of a woman. I learned, as a friend of mine once told me, that as women we have the gift to forgive what should be unforgivable. The mother, in her own screwed-up head, thought she was doing right for her kids. Meanwhile, during the case, the veteran's wife spoke of her family's struggle to survive and bring joy into the lives of their two children, in the midst of all this turmoil brought into their lives. Yet, she still forgave this mother. What an advocate for fairness. What an advocate for her husband. What an advocate for her children and even for this child caught in the middle of the case—a child she never had a chance to make part of her family. This woman is an extraordinary wife and mother.

It struck me how different these two women were from each other—the mother who felt entitled to the world and the wife of the disabled veteran, who felt only the responsibility to stand up for her family no matter what. These women represent such a dichotomy of identities and intentions, especially in the different ways they each chose to handle their hardships in life.

The defendant thought she was automatically deserving of whatever she could get out of life, using whatever unethical means were needed to get it. Her reasoning was that because she was having a hard time in life, she was entitled to compensation for her struggles. The idea that someone could make choices so far outside the realm of human decency remains extremely disturbing to me.

Especially because the veteran's wife was having an even harder time in life, as the wife of a young, otherwise healthy, handsome disabled veteran. She dealt with the emotional stress of that while also raising two little girls, and then, on top of that, she was suddenly dealing with this new, completely unnecessary, messy situation. She had it worse but she never complained. She was selfless, completely dedicated to her husband, and not afraid to speak up if it meant protecting her family. Even while dealing with this emotionally and economically draining situation, and in the midst of all the legal turmoil, her main priority was to fight on behalf of her kids and her husband. She is the least self-centered woman I have ever met. She represents all the best qualities of a woman's identity and inner strength discussed in this book. As this man's wife told her story and what she did on behalf of her family, chills ran up my spine. This case made me more than grateful for the life I live and the amazing human beings who surround me in my life.

Viewing the struggles of others makes us reflect on how both the good and bad times in our lives inspire us to appreciate, fix, and develop what we do have. This gratitude and awareness make us stronger and stronger, as we continue identifying with the good things about our lives.

I am so happy and grateful for what I have. I am happy with who I am, who my family is, and I'm proud to be the matriarch of our little family. The misery and mistakes of others automatically make us stronger and more confident in the identity and life we have created. Learning from one another should give each of us strength as women, because nobody's life is perfect.

My Verdict

It can be a rough world out there, especially if you let self-doubt be your best friend and worst enemy. Finding your strength means knowing who you are, accepting your downfalls, and celebrating your best qualities. It is all about depending on, trusting, and forgiving yourself. That is what makes you strong and leads you to make smart decisions on your own behalf.

"IN HER OWN WORDS"

I asked some smart, confident women to share their thoughts on the laws covered in this chapter. Here is what they said along with my responses.

What is the strongest piece of a woman's identity?

1. "What is strongest about my identity? I am relentless. I am courageous!"

CP: Excellent! This is the definition of strength of identity that so many other women are looking for. To develop a courageous identity you must be relentless and resilient, and persevere.

2. "As women, we can bear hardships that are unimaginable, we can stand up to injustices, and we can smile when we really want to cry."

CP: This is a unique aspect of a woman's strength of character. We find our most extraordinary strength during the toughest times and learn many valuable life lessons in the process.

CHAPTER 2

Law #2: *Celebrate Being a Woman*

The ability to celebrate being a woman is an essential part of our identity *as* women. Yet in the midst of all our other roles in life where the focus is on getting things done—projects at work, chauffeuring the kids around, doing the errands, keeping the household from falling apart, etc.—it is easy to forget the "woman" part of our identity. We trade in all the sexiest, most beautiful, most feminine, most age-defiant pieces of ourselves as women to play a role akin to a workhorse (I know, what an incredibly sexy, attractive image).

The topics in this chapter are a reminder of all the best things about being a woman. Sometimes it may seem awkward or embarrassing to remind ourselves how feminine, sexy, and beautiful we are. It may seem like vanity. But it's not. It's supporting the feminine piece of our identity.

It can also be a matter of simply forgetting this piece of our identity in the midst of the hustle and bustle. It can also be due to the never-ending battle we have with our body image. In fact, I almost listed "never being happy with your body image" as one of our most common downfalls as women. Whether it is your personal downfall or not, I want you to consider this chapter an opportunity to reconnect with all the sexiest, most feminine pieces of your identity, and above all—a reminder to *work it!*

Celebrating Your Femininity

Whenever I am around my daughter Sofia, no matter how fat, bloated, or otherwise unattractive I may feel, I am very careful not to say anything self-deprecating about my physical appearance. From her perspective I am always completely happy with my body (even during the times when I am a little iffy on the whole matter). She has taken notice of my self-assurance, even telling me, "Mommy, you have a fluffy butt." I tell her, "Yes, I do, Sofia." Then I think to myself, *Oh, God, she's right!* But then reality sets in, and I think, *Well, at least I have one.*

I think of what some women will go through to look like someone else and suddenly I love my fluffy butt! This reminds me of butt implants, and how some women try to achieve the Latin booty that seems to come naturally for sexy, self-confident ladies like Jennifer Lopez. Like Ms. Lopez, I celebrate my body because it is all mine and there is not another one like it. Nobody else wears my femininity and body image the way I do, and that is the lesson, as a woman, that I am passing on to my daughter.

As women, we all have a unique sense of self that incorporates how we view our femininity and what we think of our body image. How connected is femininity to our very identity as women? One of the definitions of the word *femininity* is "womanliness." The definition of *feminine* includes words like *sensitivity* and *gentleness*, grounded in the more obvious point that being feminine means "belonging to the female sex." Even more interesting is how being feminine is defined as "having qualities traditionally ascribed to women."

What are the qualities that you traditionally ascribe to a woman? There is an image in my mind that celebrates the message of femininity, one that mothers pass on to their daughters. I cannot say for sure if it's from a movie, a photo, a black-and-white sitcom, or purely my imagination, but this is what it looks like to me: Mom is in her bedroom getting ready for an evening out with Dad, as her daughter looks on. As Mom slips on her panty hose, a beautiful, sexy dress, and high heels, her daughter copies her, tottering around the room awkwardly and giggling in a pair of heels and a dress dragging on the floor behind her. As Mom sprays on her fancy perfume and puts on sexy red lipstick, her daughter douses herself with perfume and smears lipstick all over her face when Mom's back is turned for just a second. The daughter is learning about one aspect of femininity from her best possible teacher at an early age.

I say "one aspect," because when I use the word *femininity*, I am not just talking about the perfume, lipstick, and heels. For me, femininity is primarily about *attitude*, being comfortable in your body and exuding that quiet, soft confidence that conveys both grace and inner strength while never taking away your intelligence. These qualities make up the whole package for me.

Can we honestly say that as women, we still cherish our most womanly, feminine gifts today? From what I have seen, we are losing this bond with ourselves. I think of ladies like Grace Kelly, Marilyn Monroe, and Jackie Kennedy. They are great examples from a time when femininity was considered a sign of strength, not weakness.

We also have great role models of femininity today. We just have to look for them and make sure to point them out to our daughters. One example is the comedian Ellen DeGeneres. Ellen wears pants all the time and she is gay, beautiful, feminine, and clearly comfortable with who she is as a woman. Ellen and many other unique women are proof positive that femininity is not defined by the makeup you wear, or your sexual preferences, attire, or any other external factors. Femininity comes from the inside and is strongly rooted in our sense of identity. It is empowering to all women. There is no right or wrong way to express it. Femininity is power and totally unique to each woman who wears it in her own way.

Femininity does not contradict intelligence either. The attitude and intelligence may be at the core of your feminine identity, but that does not mean there is anything wrong with taking pride in the packaging. As women are we still buying into the old double standard that sexy and smart are contradictory? They are not and we need to stop letting society, the media, and other outdated dinosaurs convince us that they are. Sexuality absolutely does not damage our equality with men. We do not need to lose our femininity to gain equality. Putting on lipstick and a dress does not lower our IQ, nor does it hurt our chances of success. The important thing is that we all believe this and stop apologizing for being the sexy, feminine women we are.

Another reason why femininity has taken a backseat today is because we often feel as if we are too busy to take pride in the most feminine ways of expressing ourselves as women. Yes, our roles in society have expanded. As women we have more responsibilities toward more people than ever before in history. It has become much easier for the frazzled, overworked career mom running in a million different directions to toss on a pair of jeans or sweats and a T-shirt.

I understand. It is easy to become so consumed with everything else in our life that we put ourselves second. And no, I am not suggesting that you wear a dress and a string of pearls to the playground with your kids. But I also think it is all about how we wear that T-shirt and those jeans that we throw on. Just because we are working to maintain our sanity in the midst of our hectic lives does not mean we should give in, throw in the towel, and completely surrender our sense of sexiness and femininity.

I love celebrating my femininity. I don't do it for anyone else but myself, because it makes me feel good. When I am expressing the most womanly things about myself, it is not just about the makeup, costumes, and props either. Let me be perfectly clear—some of the young women who make up this new generation of "look at me" celebrity are not what I mean by celebrating your femininity.

Is it even possible to overcompensate for a lack of inner strength with over-the-top glitz, glamour, face paint, and slinky little dresses that barely qualify as clothing? When we do not have the strength of identity and comfort in our own skin to back it up, beauty props are a sign of weakness and confused priorities, not strength.

Here is an example of a case from *Cristina's Court* about a young woman, not a famous one either, who chose to prioritize her personal vanity over friendship. The story unfolded like this: Cute girls make plans for a Caribbean cruise. It's all set. All prepaid. One cute girl suddenly backs out at the last minute and gets a breast job instead. Of course, it's every cute girl's prerogative to spend her money the way she pleases. And perhaps the friendship could have been salvaged if she had known this about herself before they booked the cruise. But it was clear from the beginning of the case that this type of logic would not be present in the courtroom that day. What was present was a rather shallow young woman who could not see beyond the perceived little imperfections in the mirror—two of them, actually. I won't argue that this girl's choice to honor her femininity—well, technically her breasts—could be healthy in some circumstances. This just was not one of them. I'm not sure if she was lacking inner strength or did not particularly value her friends and the financial commitment she had made to the cruise. Or perhaps this was the only time the plastic surgeon could fit her into the schedule. We may never know. But hopefully she got that lift to her self-esteem she had been looking for.

Whether we realize it or not, expressing our femininity and sexuality is directly connected to how we see ourselves and our identity. The stronger we believe in ourselves, the more self-confidence we will have and exude. In order to find strength in our identity as women, it is essential to reconnect with the femininity that makes us women and is one of the *best* parts of being a woman.

Celebrating Your Body Image

I was watching a reality show where the goal was weight loss. This is one of many such shows on television that reflect the public's desire to lose weight, get fit, and be healthy, and I wholeheartedly support these goals. On the show, woman after woman described how sexy, confident, and beautiful she felt—on the inside. Each woman expressed her desire to work hard and get healthy so that she could feel just as great about herself on the outside as she did on the inside.

I was so excited to hear these women saying this, because it makes the point that I am trying to make with this book: We all have this seemingly elusive beautiful, sexy, smart, successful identity. But all too often we feel that it is somehow trapped deep within us and we do not know how to extract it. Or are we afraid to express the beauty within because our outside does not match what society thinks of as beautiful? I hope it is the former.

In any event, the women on this reality show talked about how they felt their identity was trapped within a fat suit. I immediately thought of the infamous social experiments done on various talk shows and entertainment television shows, where the normally thin hosts don an artificial fat suit to see how it feels to be overweight and how differently they are perceived by society. While I appreciate the intentions and empathy behind these experiments, I think in some ways they are missing the mark, and here is why.

The host with the artificial fat suit on may be able to replicate the experience of being overweight in public and even the sensation of carrying all that weight. What they will not be able to replicate, however, is the feeling expressed by the women on this reality show. They will not be able to reproduce the feeling of having their identity trapped within a body that they do not relate to as truly being them. At the end of the experiment, the host gets to remove the artificial layers. But for these women, there is nothing artificial about feeling trapped in their own skin.

I give the women on this reality show and on others like it, and the scores of other women who *don't* wait for a reality-show camera to follow them around, a lot of credit. I hope they are losing the weight for the right reasons and that they recognize the difference between who they really are on the inside—their sexy, confident, successful self— versus what is on the outside. If they are exercising their ability to get healthy and fit, while also making their outside "shell" match the powerful identity on the inside, then good for them. I hope they recognize the difference between inside and outside and don't let their weight define their inner identity. It can be quite a challenge for many of us to do this. Dissatisfaction with our body image, to the point where it affects how we feel about our identity, can make us start questioning all aspects of our body image. But if women in this situation are able to compartmentalize, then more power to them.

I know how easy it is to get caught up in the "I need to lose x pounds" syndrome. I am guilty of it too. What I have come to realize is that I am not twenty anymore. As I get older, I have learned to appreciate and love every curve, bulge, and sag of my body. After all, I am a human being, and guess what? Aging is something that happens to human beings, and there is nothing we can do to reverse it. In light of this, I am realistic about the goals I set for my body. Because I will *not* give up my wine and dessert (once or twice a week)! If I foolishly try to battle Mother Nature, guess who always wins? Knowing what I know about my body, I do my best to maintain it and keep it looking the best I can.

Finding strength in your identity means learning to accept this, and, in doing so, finding strength in your body image. Our bodies are the vessels that carry us around as people. How we treat the vessel and what we think about it are inescapably connected to the person inside. If we think of our bodies as nothing but shells, disconnected from the rest of us, then that is exactly the impression we will communicate to the world—disconnected. We cannot find strength in our complete identity if we are hiding from a whole piece of it.

Are you one of the many women who just find it hard to see themselves as sexy? Remember this: Sexy is as sexy does, so find something that makes you feel sexy. For example, exercise is a great way to get your body in shape and make you feel energized and confident. I try to exercise regularly for myself and not for anyone else. It is an incredible energy booster and stress reliever, and it keeps me in the best shape possible.

But what do we do to get our body *image* in shape? Remember that self-confidence is by far the sexiest asset a woman can project. We have all heard of "leg men," "breast men," and "butt men" in terms of the parts of the female body that certain men notice and are most attracted by. This is hilarious to me, because over and over again I watch as men are drawn to women who are self-confident and know how to "work it" with whatever God gave them—legs, breasts, butts, and everything in between. I have literally seen women of all shapes and sizes and varying levels of physical fitness bring men to their knees, simply with an almost overpowering level of self-assurance, femininity, and strength in who they are as women.

For example, we heard a case on *Cristina's Court* of a woman who had a crystal-clear understanding of who she was. The plaintiff was a large and voluptuous woman who was very proud of her body. She dressed very sexily, even provocatively by some standards. She was clearly rooted in her identity. The combination of her sexy clothing, self-confident attitude, and great smile made the men drool as she walked past them. She was proud of her body and the men took notice.

Her boyfriend was jealous of all the attention his girlfriend received on a regular basis from men. He did not like the way she dressed. It clearly brought out feelings of jealousy and insecurity in him about the image she was projecting to the world.

Their lawsuit was about the sexy clothes the woman bought. It seemed that no sooner would she buy the clothes than they would disappear. Because of his disapproving attitude toward the way she dressed, the woman was convinced that her boyfriend was throwing away or hiding the clothes as soon as she bought them. She said she was suing to get the clothes back, or at least the money she paid for them. The real purpose of the lawsuit, however, was for the woman to get her boyfriend's attention. She wanted him to understand, without a shadow of a doubt, that she loved him, and that just because she was proud of how she looked and men were drawn to her, it did not mean that she was cheating on him. She desperately wanted him to know this and accept this, and the lawsuit was her way of telling him that.

As far as the case went, we found no evidence that he took the clothes. I suggested to him that he stop being insecure with himself and their relationship. Instead, he should value his gorgeous, sexy, self-confident girlfriend, because she definitely valued herself. She had enough self-confidence to compensate for all the women who would love to be this secure with their body image.

This woman did not fit *typical* societal and media stereotypes of what is considered sexy, yet nobody in the courtroom that day would have described her as anything but. Yet for some reason, we as a society keep propping up the same tired, "perfect" stereotype of the amazing, bionic one-hundred-pound superwoman with giant breasts, a shapely butt, legs that go on forever, and a Barbie doll–size waist. Anyone who regularly follows celebrity relationship news has learned that these "perfect women" have just as much trouble with their relationships and life as the rest of us. A perfect body, just like a perfect life, is nothing but a mirage in the desert—an illusion that dissolves the moment someone comes too close.

When I think of illusions, I am reminded of my high-profile walk down the red carpet at the Daytime Entertainment Emmy Awards in Los Angeles in 2008. Television viewers may see naturally perfect, pretty people posing for the cameras, but after spending the better part of the day getting ready, I can tell you that perfection is an illusion, and "naturally pretty" takes an awful lot of work. Fortunately, I am comfortable enough in my own skin that I viewed the day as an exciting event and an opportunity to be primped and pampered.

But what was most interesting to me about my walk down the carpet that day was finding myself immersed in so many different types of women, many of whom were extremely thin. I looked upon the scene with fascination, almost as an observer (this being my first Emmy red-carpet walk and all).

First, I reflected on the pressure to look good on television. There is no denying that it is a high-pressure, image-oriented industry. Then I thought how women are this thin because they are in constant search of physical body perfection, especially when faced with the prospect of being on camera every day. I get that television adds the illusion of weight, and I understand the overall pressure within the entertainment industry to maintain a certain image. I know there was less pressure on me because there I was in my big, flowing robe sitting behind a bench. No one there could tell that I just had a steak dinner and dessert three days in a row! But I must admit, I still feel this pressure.

However, what disturbed me on the red carpet was how consumed women seemed to be with their weight, especially the younger women. It is an almost blatant insecurity. This may be partially due to the misinformed public opinion that some women, especially the ones in Hollywood, are naturally extremely thin. This is pure fantasy. The only women who are naturally stick figures are the ones drawn by animators in cartoon movies. This is because they do not need food and nourishment to live. They need only an artist's imagination. We humans need food.

I find it sad when I hear stories, whether true or not, of Hollywood industry executives who tell women who are already at a healthy weight that they need to drop *x* number of pounds. I think the executives are confusing these real-life women with cartoon women. If you do not like the way a cartoon woman looks, you can simply redraw her or otherwise mold her to fit your imagination. With real women, there are health consequences of such attempts.

I noticed how crazy the media and photographers went over the thinnest of the women, shouting out, "You look so beautiful!" This is not a commentary about the women or even the photographers. After all, the media is looking into the mirror that we are all holding up together as a society. Those photographers reflect what they think we want to see, and, at this point in history, that happens to be thinner versus thicker. At other points in history it was the opposite, and I'm sure the perception will continue to fluctuate. Therefore, it is ridiculous—in Hollywood in particular, where the mirror is the largest and sends reflections around the world—to go to the extremes that some women go to just to satisfy what they believe to be other people's expectations of them.

What I mean by the extremes is when women engage in unhealthy behaviors to become excessively thin, at a weight that is medically unsafe for them. I find it sad that women would do this to their bodies and their health. I will continue to feel this way until someone can prove to me that there are no health dangers to being extremely under one's medically recommended weight (or over, to be fair). With a father and brother who are both doctors, I have heard enough to believe that this will not be proven anytime soon.

The human body is not an outfit to be tailored. It is a living, complex, biological organism with internal processes going on that boggle the mind. If these processes fall out of balance—and they can in a split second—damage is done. We sometimes look in the mirror and think that just because we can rearrange our hair, decorate our nails, paint our faces, and remove body hair, we are in control of all the stuff on the inside too. Unless you are a surgeon, that is not the case.

Wanting to be thin, lose weight, and be healthy—and watching our weight—are just fine, within reason. There is nothing inherently wrong with these desires and behaviors. A line is crossed, however, when we make ourselves unhealthy doing it, or if we are taking these actions for someone else besides ourselves. If the body image or weight we are trying to achieve goes against what *we* truly want, especially if we are doing unhealthy things to ourselves in an attempt to achieve it, it is not okay. These are the wrong reasons to be thin or to be anything else that we do not want to be.

Besides, why would anyone want to torture her body to make it something that it is obviously not intended to be? There are some women who believe that becoming a certain weight will give them a better shot at fame or success. I have learned that at times, fame hinges on a roll of the dice: it may happen to you or it may completely pass you by. When women give up so much of their identities, and compromise their health, happiness, and priorities just because they believe that by changing the way they look, their odds of fame are somehow increased, it is just not worth it.

If our bodies are a reflection of the woman inside, how we see ourselves, and the love we have for ourselves, then the last thing we should want to do is abuse it or punish it into submission by making it conform to some ridiculously low number on the scale. When, despite the most rigorous diet and exercise program in the world, our bodies continue to bounce back to a certain weight, there is a message there. Our bodies are not betraying us. The human body is a funny thing—it ages, wrinkles, gains weight, sags, and does whatever the heck else it wants to do, because that's how it is programmed. We should respect that and find the beauty in the process, rather than fighting against it. We need to find peace with what we see in the mirror without worrying about what everyone else sees.

There is always going to be a mirror—whether it is the media, paparazzi, or even just the perceived opinions of our friends and neighbors. We cannot change the fact that there is a mirror. But we can work together to change what we see in the reflection. And while the gradual shift has begun to do that, we can choose as individual women to put our own self-images and personal priorities above anything in the societal mirror that is not a reflection of us as individuals.

When we look at what society is reflecting and see women who do not look like us, who cares? They do not live our lives and do not have our identities, so who the heck cares if they don't look like us? Images from Hollywood are exactly that, yet so many women take them to heart as so much more than that. They use the images as a method of comparison and an excuse to feel bad about themselves.

The whole scene on the red carpet and all my observations actually made me feel *better* about myself. I realized that I was technically the same clothing size as those women, and yet my body shape was a little curvier, with biceps and a butt, so I looked big next to them. It is so easy for many women to allow situations like this (red carpet or in everyday life) to make them feel bad about their own body image. Instead, I chose to use it as an opportunity to celebrate my body image and everything unique about myself.

The lesson I learned from my red-carpet rendezvous is that it is essential to maintain a good sense of who we are and what we stand for. If we do not, a scene like that sort of escape from reality can carry us away and make us start needlessly doubting ourselves. If we are not careful, we can talk ourselves into believing in an impossible standard of perfection that does not exist.

So who established this standard of one-hundred-pound "perfection" anyway? This image is completely opposite what a woman is biologically designed to be—curvy, voluptuous, and strong. Whether we are starving ourselves to "perfection" or simply fighting against those ten extra pounds that we are convinced are the *only thing* keeping us from true happiness, the struggle is not worth it, and none of us will ever find true happiness that way. It is just too hard to live a fulfilling, satisfying life while constantly fighting and doubting ourselves and our body image, or letting others plant the seeds of idealism in our minds. As women, we need to stop letting people dictate to us what the ideal woman is. *You* are the only person who can dictate what *your* ideal is.

What is your realistic perception of yourself? When you look in the mirror do you see the positives or negatives first? (Quick, answer before you censor yourself.) Now determine what, in a perfect world, you would physically change about yourself if you could. How would those physical changes strengthen your identity—the core of who you are? If you have an answer to that question that you are satisfied with and feel comfortable with, then please don't let anyone take that away from you. If making a change to your outward appearance will strengthen the core of your identity and give you a renewed level of self-confidence, then please, by all means, do what you feel in your heart you have to do to feel good about yourself.

While loving ourselves first, always, and in spite of our perceived flaws and imperfections is hard to do, it is critical to our self-worth and our opinion of ourselves. We put expectations on ourselves that we will never realistically be able to live up to. When we try—over and over again—to live up to an impossible and, quite frankly, unhealthy standard of perfection, it only damages what we have successfully created so far in our lives. Nurture your identity by finding strength in your own uniqueness and your accomplishments (no matter how big or small). We need to stop competing with ourselves, because we will never win.

What if we just stopped? What if we just stopped questioning ourselves, stopped criticizing ourselves, stopped making those little self-deprecating ("I hate my body—just kidding") "jokes" about ourselves and others? Imagine a world where women stopped inflicting this type of torture on themselves (and, let's face it, the people around them too). What are we waiting for? I wonder at what point in our lives we stop being harsh with ourselves, stop competing with unrealistic expectations, and start enjoying our lives.

While you are holding yourself to these impossible standards, remember from my "fluffy butt" story that as a mom, you are being watched. I am talking to all women, especially to the moms out there who are like me, and have a perceptive little girl who hears every single thing I say about myself in her presence. I am her mentor in that regard, and I have to be careful of what I say all the time. The last thing I want is for my gorgeous little girl to grow up believing that she is imperfect in any way as a woman.

Celebrating Your Age

What if I told you that the concept of age is more about perception than about the number of candles on your birthday cake? Would you believe me? If you think about it, this is a true statement.

Societal perceptions about age change so quickly that I wonder if someone is playing a cruel joke on us. How we feel about ourselves as women at one age is apparently supposed to be entirely inappropriate at another age. I don't buy it. And I just don't see how we as women are supposed to take any of this too seriously. Some of us fret over every passing birthday as if the piece of our identity containing all our femininity, sexiness, and body image is being extinguished when we blow out the candles.

It does not have to be this way. Just as we are all in control of our self-perception, our body image, and how feminine and sexy we are, we are also empowered to create our own perceptions about age. Despite what outside parties such as society and media would have us believe, we are the judge and jury in the case of age and what it means.

Besides, even if we wanted to, how could we keep up with how society and the media perceive beauty and youth? It is silly to think that as women we are going to somehow do something about what people think about our age. Are we supposed to hop in a time machine and travel in reverse, or just feel bad about ourselves for getting older and losing our desirable youthfulness?

On top of that, the way youth is perceived and even how it is defined continues to change with each generation, and sometimes with each new television season. Teenagers used to be considered children, and now they dress and act like miniadults in training. I have lost track of whether thirty is the new twenty, the old forty, or something else entirely. At one time, women in their forties were considered spring chickens; at another, they were grandmothers; and now we are sexy cougars, stealing all the young guys and exerting our sexiness on society more powerfully than ever before. The list of how age is a continuously changing perception by society goes on and on.

Perception of age also fluctuates from person to person. For instance, we heard a case on *Cristina's Court* that was heralded by the entrance into the courtroom of one of the most self-confident, sexiest litigants to appear on our show and probably in the history of all television court shows. This woman knew how to work it, and that was exactly what she did from the moment she entered the courtroom. Heads turned, men salivated, and I think I even caught Renard giving her a second look (and he's as straight an arrow as they come).

The reason I am using this sexy lady as an example of age is that she was going on sixty years old. Believe me, this self-assured woman's age was the last thing on the minds of the men in the courtroom that day. She was clearly unaffected by her age. She celebrated every piece of her identity and loved doing it.

Unfortunately, there was another piece of this woman's identity that was less of a celebration, especially for the defendant, a much younger man who was madly in love with her. Actually, he had one magnificent obsession in this world, and it was her. He promised her the world and she told him she wanted two. For a while he was able to deliver, and his lady was content. When the money finally ran dry and he could no longer fulfill his promises to provide her with anything her heart desired (while his heart desired only her), she sued him for what she, in her self-entitled mind, considered to be false promises. The poor guy was clearly still in love with her and mesmerized by the way she worked everything feminine about herself, including her age, with no shame. It's just too bad she didn't have any shame when it came to demanding the world from this man.

Despite the lessons learned from women like this who know how to work it at any age, according to some people it's all downhill after you reach a certain age (fill in your own arbitrary number if it makes you feel better). And to think that old age used to mean experience and wisdom, and in some cultures it still does. I am also reminded that the most admired and photographed trees on the planet are the ones that have lasted and survived the elements the longest. Yet, as humans, the models who end up on magazine covers are nothing but immature "saplings" (if we are comparing women to trees, that is).

I will admit that when I hear this garbage about youth meaning beauty and getting older as somehow depleting the beauty supply, I cringe and laugh at the same time. Because I remember being a little girl impatient to be a teenager, a teenager who could not wait until adulthood, and then suddenly an adult wondering what happens next. I was somehow convinced that the age I was looking forward to at that time—sixteen, twenty-one, thirty—was the magic age where I would suddenly become a beautiful, sexy, confident woman. In my mind, I saw women all around me blossoming into womanhood at these ages and I was eager to join them.

Although there is no "magic age," my thirtieth birthday celebration gave me pause for reflection. I was to celebrate my birthday with family and friends at my favorite restaurant. I arrived at the restaurant early and was the first one there. As it turned out, there was a reason that I showed up first. Sitting alone at the big, empty table, I reflected on some recent events having to do with age.

I had run into a friend from high school, and as we reminisced I suddenly felt younger than I had in my life so far. At one point I felt as if I were actually back in high school! I felt younger and, according to the comments I had been receiving lately, I looked younger too. My friends had recently started telling me, "You look younger every time I see you, Cristina!" And since I have very genuine, up-front friends, I had no reason to doubt them. Besides, what they were saying was completely matching up with how I had been feeling. I felt younger, but at the same time I recognized the gradual metamorphosis I had been going through starting in my late twenties.

Back then I was still so busy trying to be the best that I was not enjoying my life in general. Looking back, I realized how my quest to be the best started in law school, when that woman, in her own way, told me I wasn't good enough to make the grade in the legal profession. My journey may have started as a way of proving her wrong, as well as the unknown others who, in my mind, were thinking the same thing about me. But even after graduating law school and giving that speech in front of my class, I was still on some sort of mission to silence my critics and prove that I was the best. What I realized, as I progressed through my twenties, was that I was my worst critic, and the only person I was battling was myself.

Sitting at that big, empty table at my favorite restaurant, waiting for my thirtieth birthday celebration to begin, I then reflected on some realizations about age, professionally and personally, that I had recently been mulling over. I had realized that one of the keys to being the best professional I could be had nothing to do with these invisible battles against faceless enemies and critics. At the age of thirty I finally appreciated that the key to my work was just being myself and learning to personally connect with the facts of each case at hand, without trying to prove anything. At any age, when I was myself I was always at my best and smartest. I immediately saw that this self-confidence had led to how much I was finally enjoying my work, and in all likelihood it was keeping me young too.

When we are comfortable with who we are and enjoy what we do, age becomes just a number. So, as the number changes from year to year, we gain more and more self-confidence: We walk taller, we smile more, and we laugh more. These are the things that keep us young, and the more we realize this, the more it shows. When I turned thirty, I really tuned into who I was and have never looked back.

As I have passed from decade to decade there has not been some extreme makeover of my outside either. The compliments I receive that "you look younger every time I see you" are reflections of what I am feeling on the inside. I have grown into my identity as a woman and learned that all the beautiful, sexy confidence I was once looking for was developing from within myself the whole time.

The unfortunate irony here is that some people believe that a woman's "shell" is at its most beautiful in her twenties, when her iden- tity is still actively developing through all kinds of wonderful learning experiences. I personally started feeling the *most* confident with my identity as a woman when I hit my mid- to late twenties and then into my thirties. For the first time in my life I was not waiting to arrive at some mystery age or life landmark, and ironically, today I feel younger than ever before. I finally feel like I can fill out every square inch of my skin with inner strength and confidence. Obviously this is different for every woman, but please take a moment to look at who you are, all the things about you that give you plenty of reasons to be sexy and confi- dent. I would hate for you to miss this amazing moment of realization that has nothing to do with a chronological number.

Because if we are waiting for a magic pill that makes our inner confidence sync up with the brief heartbeat of time when our physical body reaches its biological peak, then we may be waiting for eternity.

We cannot control biology, Mother Nature, and everything else that makes our bodies do what they do as they age the way they are supposed to.

This lesson was reinforced in me by my father and brother, who frequently deal with patients with varying points of view on health and what it means to age. Interestingly enough, my father's elderly patients have the healthiest life views. He has observed in them that when you act young you stay young, and that while aging is biological, getting old is entirely a state of mind. Now if we could only get this through our heads a lot earlier in life!

Let's stop obsessing over that little number that simply indicates how many years we have survived and thrived on this earth. Our age should be a badge of honor, showing how long we have overcome many odds while achieving many successes in life. And that realization is a beautiful thing.

Celebrating Your Beauty

Femininity is the physical expression of the attitude, sexiness, and self-confidence that comes from being a woman. Body image is what we see when we look in the mirror and how we feel about it. Age is the number of years we have had to master these ideas. Beauty occurs when we come to the realization that our powerful expressions of femininity combined with our positive body image make us all truly extraordinary women.

Some women I know find it hard to view photographs or videos of themselves, or even hear their own voice on an answering machine. How funny that most of us don't look or sound like we do in our own minds! I think this is one of God's ways of reminding us that we only *think* we've got it all figured out. Fortunately, the joke is evened out, because generally speaking, most of us do not see nearly the amount of beauty and attributes in ourselves that others see in us. I wish there were a special mirror where we truly could see how others see us. This would be a major beauty aid and self-esteem booster, and much cheaper than most of the other beauty aids on the market.

Because when people admire beauty, they are taking note of the complete package, from the inside out. They are also not focusing on all the flaws that we have talked ourselves into seeing in the mirror, simply from staring into it every day. Remember the fairy tale witch who used to constantly stare into her magic mirror, daring the voice inside to tell her who was more beautiful than she was? Most of us seem to have the opposite affliction. We ask our mirrors to find all the reasons that we are *not* beautiful. Let's pretend to be an evil witch for once and look for all the things that make us beautiful.

Beauty celebrates femininity, body image, and the love we feel for ourselves as women. True beauty transcends age, imperfections, comparisons with others, and the fantasy of being perfect. This is why there is only so far one can go in purchasing beauty. Age does not have a reverse gear, although it sometimes wears a mask. There is also only so far we can go in attempting to defy gravity.

Products and procedures that try to do this are certainly not enhancing beauty. However, if they somehow make you feel better about yourself, I won't try to talk you out of getting that face, boob, or butt lift. As long as you realize that the most important work you can do to enhance your identity does not involve a scalpel, a needle, or ending up in credit card debt from endless jars of masks, lotions, and "miracle" cures. The only miracle is realizing the self-confidence and courage it takes to see the beauty that is *already* there and cannot be found in an operating room or pharmacy.

It is up to each woman to look in the mirror and find what makes her beautiful. No two women are beautiful for the same reason, and each woman's journey to this realization is as unique as her identity. The best day to start your journey toward realizing that you are beautiful is today.

My Verdict

Being comfortable with who you are and in the body that God gave you is a trait of an empowered woman that reflects the kind of quiet confidence in yourself that exudes grace and inner strength. Remember that the beauty and simplicity of life lies in being proud of who *you* are—and being who *you* are is sexy.

"IN HER OWN WORDS"

I asked some smart, confident women to share their thoughts on the laws covered in this chapter. Here is what they said, along with my responses.

What are the most valuable aspects of your femininity as a woman?

1. "I think we are worth far more than we think as women. We underestimate our worth and the best things about being women."

CP: Learning to stop underestimating our self-worth is the key to being empowered with ourselves and our identity.

2. "I think that what I value most about my femininity is that I am very sensitive, which is a great help to me in many ways. Of course, it can be hurtful too, but when I think about it, then it is a great tool when I write, sing, and act. I also believe that my sensitivity is one of the reasons why I have a great intuition/sixth sense. Another thing about my femininity I value a lot is my effeminate character, which many men like. I think it is great to be a woman, and I think that every woman should be proud of being a woman, just like every man should feel proud of being a man. These mysteries are true magic."

CP: It is interesting how she calls these things mysteries, because they are not mysteries at all. They are things that we have known all along. If we tuned in to them, and tuned in often, they would no longer be mysterious and magical. They would be part of our everyday lives. Then perhaps we would not have so many problems fully embracing this piece of our identities as women.

CHAPTER 3

Law #3: *Take a Risk*

When Not to Say No

When I was offered the opportunity to host my first court show on local television in Los Angeles, I was afraid of the whole idea of being on television, and I initially said *no*. But I ultimately felt that if I didn't at least show up, I would regret it for the rest of my life. Besides, I told myself, at the very least I would have a great story to tell my children someday. Secretly, I was terrified of what would come from the screen test.

I was so strong in many ways, so why was I afraid of this? After thinking about it, I realized that like so many women everywhere, I was not afraid of the opportunity for success, but was afraid of rejection and failure.

No. How can one little two-letter word cause so much trouble for women? Using it can make us seem disagreeable (or worse, depending on the situation), and failing to use it can make us into pushovers. For these reasons and more, I have labeled the word *no* as an excellent example of a double-edged sword.

It all seems so simple. Someone asks us to do something and, for our own reasons (whether good or bad), we don't want to. We know what we have to do. We know what we should do. We know we need to say no. But before the little word can make it out of our mouth, our inner voice flies into a frenzy of doubt, anxiety, and second-guessing: *What will this person think of me if I say no? Do I even want to do this? Of course I want to do this. I'm sure I can fit it into my schedule if I try. I'm being ridiculous. I should just say yes and be done with it. What if this person thinks I'm being impolite and then tells everyone else that I'm a rude person? What will people think if I just go around saying no all the time like this?*

All of this drama over one little two-letter word. There are, of course, right reasons to say no: reasons that respect your best interests. I will get to those. But for now, let's figure out together why, as women, we have such trouble saying no.

When you ask a man if he wants to do something and he does not want to do it, how long does it take him to say no? Based on my observations, it is along the lines of warp speed and measurable only by NASA scientists.

No problem whatsoever, case closed, moving on, and what's for dinner? While we women often struggle internally with all the possible outcomes of saying no, men just see it as giving a simple answer to a simple question. Picture the same situation two different ways.

Guy #1: Hey, man, you wanna go skiing this weekend? I got a cabin up at Tahoe and I'm getting a group together.

Guy #2: No, but thanks anyway. I got plans. Some other time?

Guy #1: Sure, no problem. Let's go get some beer and burgers.

Guy #2: Sounds good.

Woman #1: Do you want to go skiing this weekend? I've rented a cabin and made all the arrangements. Everyone will be there.

Woman #2 (after the paralytic hesitation passes and she finishes frantically biting her lip): Actually . . . I can't. I'm sorry; I wish I could. I already made other plans . . . I mean, I could try to get out of them, but . . . I'm sorry. Are you mad at me?

Woman #1 (in an offended tone): Well, if you don't want to go why don't you just say so and I'll invite someone who does!

Okay, I will admit I may have exaggerated both of these situations into television sitcom skits. But hopefully you get my point. This is the exact same situation. Woman #2 is not trying to be impolite, any more than Guy #2 is. But look at what a little altered perception and our natural instinct to take things personally can turn into.

Why are woman afraid of the word *no*? One reason is that, as naturally analytical creatures, we feel that every *no* requires an in-depth, watertight explanation that would withstand cross-examination by Supreme Court justices. There is absolutely no need for us to feel this need to justify everything we say and do to anyone else. In five years, nobody will remember that you passed up the opportunity to organize your child's school fund-raiser. Nobody will still be holding grudges against you for this. Even if they do, it is your prerogative to brush off such personal misjudgments.

It is so important for us to realize and accept that other people will sometimes feel inconvenienced when we say no, simply because our *no* may put more work on their plate or because they are disappointed or for some other personal reason that is not our fault. You know what? They will get over it, and so should we. This seems like such a simple concept, and yet one that escapes so many of us when we are actually *in* the situation. In that moment, it feels like we are being permanently judged as the worst kind of person for saying no. Whether it happens in the workplace or the community, we think that we are not being team players. In personal situations, we think we are being rude or negative. No matter how the situation is playing out in reality, it is always much worse in our minds. Our inner voices are screaming that these labels will follow us forever.

So what if they will? Let us pretend that all the things people are thinking about us, just because we said no, are true. Why should we care? To avoid the possibility of social stigma, are we willing to say yes to absolutely everything that everyone asks of us for the rest of our lives? It is not worth going against our own wishes and better judgment just because in our minds we feel emotionally pressured or bullied into backing down and going along with the crowd.

We would then be everyone else's puppet to push around just because we are too afraid to say no. On top of that, in five years they *still* won't remember who ran that school fund-raiser. Yes, in the moment, the consequences of standing up for ourselves may seem totally flipped around from the reality of the situation. It may seem a lot more serious than it is. Remember that nothing is permanent, even someone's opinion. Knowing this, and knowing everything else we know about ourselves, is it really worth putting ourselves through the back-and-forth of it all? We need to learn to accept our decisions, say no without fear of repercussions, tell ourselves, "Who cares?" and move on.

Another reason that we are afraid to say no may be based on our upbringing as women, depending on how each one of us was raised. The fact is that many of us were told to be nice and polite, which, for some reason, seemed to be a direct contradiction to ever uttering the word *no*.

I may have learned this just from observing my mother. She was the backbone of our family. She was the one who had to always be there, ready to take care of everyone's needs at a moment's notice. She had to keep the house in order, the kitchen always running, and, similar to my father, she basically had to be on call twenty-four/seven for anything our family needed. There was no question that she had to say yes to everything. She was the central cog in the machine that was our household. If she stopped, so would the machine.

Never saying no did not take away from my mother's strength in the least. In her case, she was placing her family's needs first, and that meant being the family's *yes* person. Do not forget also that this was a different time, and many women played this central role within their families.

However, as young girls watching our mothers, it was easy to carry the lesson with us into adulthood that women say yes because they *have* to say yes, and the world comes crashing down if they say no. Add that to the polite, soft-spoken, agreeable image of a "lady" from that period in time and the lesson is cemented—nice ladies *do not* say no.

Back then, women who *did* go around saying no all the time were often characterized as selfish, rude, and generally disagreeable. We were taught that being agreeable is interchangeable with being feminine and desirable, generous, kind, and nurturing women. Do you remember any of these as qualities of femininity as I described earlier in the book? Of course not, because it is simply not true! As I mentioned, at the core of femininity is inner strength, and with that strength comes a strong point of view. A woman with a strong point of view will say yes when she wants to say yes, and no when it is right for her to say no, without the fear of being labeled as a bad person. She also will not believe overly simplified stereotypes that characterize *yes* girls as good and *no* girls as bad.

When men say no they are usually commended for defending their integrity and taking a stand. We should be able to say no just as easily as we say yes, without all the psychodrama, and without feeling like we either have to be a total *yes* person or a total *no* person.

When to Say No

I wish I had an all-encompassing, dramatic personal story to tell you about how I found the courage to say no to a request or a new role in life as a way of protecting my sanity. The truth is that not saying no when I probably should, because my life is bursting at the seams and cannot handle another "yes, of course I will do it," is one of my greatest personal weaknesses, while also one of my best personal strengths. I know that if I could learn to use this powerful little word more often, my life might not be as beautifully hectic as it often gets.

But there are good reasons to say no. It is easy for us to believe that if we say no, as in, "No, I don't *want* to do this," we are saying that we *cannot* do something. We believe that people are somehow looking at how far we have come as women and throwing back in our face, "I thought you were all invincible, and now you're saying you can't do this?" Let's be rational about this. When we choose to say no for our own reasons of self-respect and self-preservation, we are not saying we cannot do something. We are saying, with absolute inner strength in our convictions, that we *choose* not to.

Because we willingly accept so many different roles in life, it is very easy to find ourselves overextended without even realizing that we were extended in the first place. Sometimes we forget how to draw the line. For the overburdened woman, *no* can be the most liberating word in the world. There are basically two ways of looking at this: It can either be a downfall that we spread ourselves too thin, or a positive character trait that we have the ability to multitask and do many projects at once. Regardless of how you look at it, realizing what one can and cannot do, and then following through on that realization, are the signs of a very strong woman. We know what our limitations are, just like we know what our strengths are. When we are being honest with ourselves, we know what we can and cannot do, and that information should be the basis for all our decisions.

But the double-edged sword definitely cuts both ways. In life there are no black-and-white answers about anything. In a woman's life this is even truer. How could it not be, with the number of hats we wear? Instead of seeing this as confusing or contradictory, as long as I keep reality in check I choose to celebrate the beautiful, layered complexity that adds to my strength as a woman. If it is a woman's prerogative to change her mind, then why *should* we be simple creatures? Embrace your contradictions.

My contradiction is that I can sometimes simultaneously feel the urge to say yes and no at the same time. As I said before, it is one of my greatest weaknesses and strengths. The important thing is to put our decisions in perspective and not to let anyone tell us that *no* means *can't.*

Life Outside Your Comfort Zone

I have a confession to make: It was once extremely hard for me to take chances. This may surprise you and others who know me and have observed all the risks I have taken in my life, especially professional ones, that have for the most part paid off. This does not mean that I have *always* found it easy to take risks. At one time in my life it was hard for me to take risks and step outside my comfort zone. In some ways and in some situations it still is. But the older I get, the more I learn that taking risks challenges me, and from challenges come strength and the awareness of what I know and what I don't know.

When we take ourselves for a test drive and take a risk, we find out what we are made of.

Nevertheless, even with the risks I take, I remain at my core a very organized, structured, and methodical person. I admitted earlier in the book how perfectionism is a downfall that I am constantly working on in myself. In a sense, this behavior is a direct result of my need to control as much as possible about my busy, hectic life. I have no one to blame except myself, and honestly, I wouldn't have it any other way. I love my crazy life!

The busier my life gets, it seems, the more and more work and responsibilities I willingly accept. Call me a workaholic if you want, because I love to work. It makes me tick. But I never take on more than I can handle, because I know my capabilities and my work capacity. I understand my strengths and weaknesses, and most of the time I know how to say no (this has been a learning process in my life). When I take a risk, I take the ones that will expand my identity and help me grow.

Each one of us obviously has our own personal motivations for doing good work, and our own style and method of getting it all done. I have learned about myself that having a lot to do makes me get compartmentally organized and raises my game.

Exerting control and structure over my life is my way of getting things done and holding on to my sanity in the process. I want you to keep all of this in mind as you read the following story about what happened when I stepped outside of the structured life I am used to, and took a huge risk. Hopefully it inspires you to take similar risks in your own life.

Now I present a typical Saturday evening in the life of Cristina Perez. Picture it: Me, onstage at a local Los Angeles theater in a *Saturday Night Live*–style comedy sketch in front of a packed house. In one hilarious sketch, I played a woman trying to explain to her husband why having sex with aliens wasn't technically cheating, because they weren't really people. Was this some kind of bizarre dream? Looking out into the darkness of the theater and listening to the laughter, I reflected on how the heck I got myself into this situation in the first place.

My role as comedy show host for an evening was born after I did a media interview at the ACME Comedy Theatre in Los Angeles. The studio's public relations person for their comedy show approached me about guest-hosting their live sketch show. I am not an actress, I have no performance training, and there is no evidence that I'm the next Lucille Ball. I had every reason in the world to say no. So of course I blurted out yes before he finished asking the question. Was I crazy? What would possess me to do such a thing? Believe me, I was just as surprised as anyone when the word yes came flying out of my mouth.

Based on my perfectionist, structured life I just described to you, for me to even have considered doing a comedy show—of all things—was ridiculous. It was a choice that was completely outside the controlled life I am used to. I put my life on hold to take a risk and confront a different fear—actually enjoying it! Hosting this live comedy show was the exact opposite of my life—the way it used to be, anyway. Thankfully, I am not as hard on myself as I used to be.

When this opportunity came along, I was at a point in my life where I felt like I had nothing to lose and everything to gain. I thought, *Why not?* and dove into the deep end of the pool. In the days leading up to the event I was a nervous wreck and at times wondered how I would pull off my new role as comedienne for an evening. But I never regretted my decision—not for a minute.

It ended up being a fabulous evening and a great experience all around. Challenging myself in this way made me test and then reinvent myself. I found a new, previously undiscovered piece of myself. Taking risks like this makes us realize that we are capable of so much more than we ever thought we were. My ACME comedy experience was also a great reminder that, as women, our identities are constantly evolving, and pushing through such an overpowering urge to say no is a big step in that personal growth. I needed that out-of-the-box experience.

Some of the best things in my life have come from resisting the urge to say no. In my professional life in law, as a business owner, television judge, and author, not saying no has liberated me and pushed me to take risks.

In my personal life, I never felt ready to have kids, so I kept procrastinating and thinking it was something I could do later. At the time in my life when I thought this, I was completely career driven. I felt the personal need to be the best in my field, make the money to back it up, and above all, work, work, work until there was no more work to be done. Even though I knew I wanted to have a family, I kept putting it next on my list of priorities. I kept saying no to the idea without really thinking about when I planned on saying yes.

That all changed one day when I was driving home from court on a Los Angeles freeway and was involved in a horrible car accident. My car flipped over again and again across five lanes of the freeway and bounced off the center divider. It is true what they say about your life passing in front of your eyes. I thought I was going to die—I was convinced of it. But shockingly nothing happened to me except the rude awakening that my priorities were in the wrong place. I realized that it was not a question of whether or not I wanted a family. Of course I wanted one. But I was so stuck on trying to be the best, and for whom? I wondered what I was trying to prove, anyway. In my headstrong quest to try to be the best at everything, tripping over my own downfall of perfectionism, I wasn't enjoying my life. How can we give of ourselves if we don't have a clear idea of who we are and what we have to offer? I realized I had one life to live and I had better start living it right!

After I experienced my rude awakening and finally confronted my own fears, I had my beautiful Sofia, and being a mother has been by far the greatest experience of my life. Pushing through the urge to say no has opened up a whole new life for me, by taking the fear away from living.

Our natural instincts are to protect ourselves and play it safe. It is human nature. Of course we want to play it safe in life and avoid rocking the boat. We want to be in nurturing, caring relationships without any problems. Saying no is a natural protective instinct to ensure that safety.

However, there is something to be said about challenging human nature once in a while. Think about firefighters who fight all natural survival mechanisms as human beings and run toward instead of away from fire. Think of soldiers who run toward deadly gunfire instead of away from it. We should try to challenge ourselves whenever we come across a situation where *no* seems like the easiest, most obvious answer to the question at hand. We can find the strength to push past the inner dialogue and say, *Yes, this is what I'm going to do.* Ask yourself, *What's the very worst thing that could happen?* When you face the worst-case scenario, suddenly the question at hand no longer seems as terrifying. Find the strength in yourself to believe you can do it, and do it.

Looking closely at our desire to say no makes us aware of what we want to do, what we don't want to do, and why. When we are confronted with an opportunity where saying no is an option, we are challenged to ask ourselves hard questions and forced to make a decision by examining our values, beliefs, and goals. Without confronting our desire to escape by saying no, we might never gain this level of awareness.

This reminds me that things are not always meant to be easy in life, and sometimes they're just downright hard to face. Even during the worst times in my life, the fact that I have confronted challenges without running away has let me know that everything was going to be okay. The more we resist the urge to say no, the more we grow and evolve as human beings.

Living inside our comfort zone, within a set of safe boundaries that we have created, is a pretty easy choice. Within those boundaries, it is perfectly acceptable to do something because we can, because there is really no decision involved, and because it is just an easy choice. There are no obstacles in our comfort zone. But at the first sign of any kind of obstacle, real or imagined, the first words that pop into our heads are, *Oh, no, I can't do this!* This sequence of events almost always slams shut the door of opportunity.

What if we could gain this kind of awareness before being confronted with these types of on-the-spot situations? What if we could gain an awareness of our comfort zone, boundaries, fears, self-imposed limitations, and perceived obstacles before being confronted with a big decision? With a little self-reflection we *can*. We can make the choice to think about these things sooner rather than later. If we answer these questions ahead of time and get to know ourselves on this level, we are more likely to say yes than no when thrust into a situation where an answer is required. Asking ourselves these questions will create more opportunities than we ever would have embraced otherwise.

I have also realized on a personal level that as we get older, we are inspired to take more risks and put ourselves out there more, whether it means success or failure. For me it has become easier to live outside of my comfort zone for the sake of my daughter and the legacy that I will leave for her. I want her to learn about strength, fearlessness, and the benefits of taking risks from my example. Isn't this inherent to our identity as women—setting a courageous example for future generations of how strong a woman can be when she takes risks? Every time we take a chance, whether for personal growth or to make things better for our families, it increases our inner strength and the strength of our identity as women.

I know some of us prefer to stay in the shallow end of the pool, where life is safe and predictable. We may associate taking risks with being an irresponsible woman, wife, and mother. One of the worst perceived insults one woman can hurl at another woman is the accusation of being irresponsible. This affects us on a deep, emotional level, as it should. This also makes sense because as women we have many responsibilities to many people, with our families at the top of that list. But taking risks is not irresponsible if we do it mindfully and consider the consequences. It is irresponsible only if we intentionally do something while knowing that there could be catastrophic consequences and choosing to ignore that possibility. Most risks, no matter how potentially catastrophic we have built them up to be in our minds, do *not* fall under the category of irresponsible decisions. It is up to each of us as individuals to weigh the pros and cons and figure out the difference. Do not let fear masquerade as an irresponsible decision.

My Verdict

No is a powerful word. It can be debilitating but also liberating. Knowing the difference means allowing your courage to guide you. Life is an ongoing education, and the best way to advance from level to level is to keep taking chances and learn to live outside your comfort zone.

"IN HER OWN WORDS"

I asked some smart, confident women to share their thoughts on the laws covered in this chapter. Here is what they said, along with my responses.

Why do you think women are often reluctant to say no?

1. "Not all women have a backbone or a mind of their own to speak up and say what's on their mind, much less say, 'No!'"

CP: Enough said!

Continued

2. "A lot of women are misguided into thinking that they have to please everyone. Many women have it ingrained that being agreeable equates to being feminine, and that a good, desirable woman is kind and generous. Saying no doesn't make us bad people. There should be no guilt associated with saying no—it doesn't make us mean."

CP: That's right. At some point we have to put ourselves first. Because if we continually try to please others, how will we know if we are happy with ourselves? We have to make ourselves complete before we can please others.

PART III
Identifying with Others

CHAPTER 4

Law #4: *Date Wisely*

W hen I first met my husband, Christopher, it wasn't exactly "thunderbolt from the sky" love at first sight. To be honest, one of the first things that did catch my attention was his behind (he's got a nice one). Is that a bad thing that I noticed my future husband's backside before his front? Anyway, sometimes you have only a moment to take in a first impression. That just happened to be what I took in during that moment. In my defense, I was awfully busy with school. In law school, with the academic pressure and expectations constantly surrounding you, the last thing you think about is relationships. My friends had the exact opposite attitude. They had been relentless about trying to set me up with Christopher from day one.

For those of you who have not met my husband, let me paint a mental picture for you. Christopher is a macho New York Puerto Rican, a.k.a. Nuyorican, from the Bronx, but without a typical New

York accent. I have found very few locations that require a *the* in front of the location name as much as the Bronx. Think about it—have you ever heard anyone say, "I'm from Bronx"? When you come from a place significant enough to require a *the* introduction, you need a significant personality to back it up. A place with that much character also tends to develop characters. I knew from our first meeting that Christopher had that personality, and he is definitely a character. With his abrasive, quick, dry way of communicating, if you do not know him he may come off as condescending and rude. But I had realized that he was not trying to be rude at all. That's just how he is. He is bluntly frank and straightforward.

I had to remind myself of this just the other day, when I asked my husband if he could bring me a glass of water and he blatantly answered, "No." This is not a reflection of how he feels about me, and no, he was not mad at me at the time. I had simply asked him a question and, as he saw it, he was answering honestly that no, he was not currently in a position that would facilitate walking into the kitchen and bringing me a glass of water. He was watching a show called *The Big Break* on the Golf Channel. This show is like *American Idol* for golfers, and you would think that as an *American Idol* fan I might have some sympathy for his predicament. Instead, I got a little pissed because I thought, *I would bring him a glass of water!* But I had to laugh, because for all his minor flaws, I see twice as many things that I love about him. The pros definitely outweigh the cons.

Anyway, back to how I met this character with the great backside named Christopher from the Bronx. Just as good, loyal girlfriends do, my friends had ignored my halfhearted pleas about not wanting to be set up, and invited Christopher to one of our study groups. I learned from this experience that as long as they are not overstepping their boundaries, there is something to be said about friends who are stubbornly convinced that they know what is best for you, no matter how much you insist that you know what you are doing. As it turned out, they knew what they were doing with this one.

Christopher thought so too, because during the study group he asked me if I wanted to go out with him afterward. I immediately blurted out, "Oh, I can't. I'm busy; I have plans. I hope you understand. Oh, I'm so sorry; I wish I could, but I just can't." Remember what I said in the ski trip dialogue about all the excuses we women make rather than simply saying no?

This was not the truth. I did not just have "plans." I had a date. I immediately felt awful. My womanly sixth sense was screaming at me to fix this. Because I felt that maybe something was different about this man. So I called him back an hour later and called myself out. I said, "I'm sorry; I lied to you." I admitted to him that I actually had a date.

While I was unsure about how Christopher would react, I was a bit surprised at my own openness. But in a way I was proud of myself for being so honest with him. As it turned out, he was also pleased with my straightforward approach. He later told me that he admired the fact that I was not afraid to be honest with him, even if I had told him I was going out with another guy. He liked that I didn't feel the need to be coy. Instead of being jealous at the idea of my going on other dates, he was just impressed. Call me crazy, but maybe I acted this way because I *knew* he was the one. Maybe that's why I had the courage to just be myself from the very beginning.

My love story introduces some of the most important dating principles that I want you to take to heart: being honest, not playing games, saying what you mean, being true to who you are, and always, always, always exhibiting your strength of identity.

Here is an example of a woman I met who exhibited incredible strength of identity. I call her the "I don't date" girl. I met her while I was in Las Vegas on business and went out to dinner with some friends.

One of my friends, a Vegas local, was accompanied by a female friend who had flown in from California to spend some time with him. While they were already friends, they were not yet dating. As the girl put it, they were simply getting to know each other. And for the record, she was staying in the guest room at his house. This was not a date. But some of the other guys in our group didn't quite see it that way. As much as she kept insisting, "This is not a date," they smirked and exchanged knowing winks, theorizing that since she got on a plane and flew to Vegas for a few days, it *must* be a date and more. To them, that was the only reasonable explanation.

I disagreed with the peanut gallery based on the facts of the case. Most important, both the woman and her date were on the same page as far as expectations. They had communicated to each other honestly (bravo!), and they agreed that the time they spent in Vegas together was strictly to get to know each other in a no-pressure, nondate situation like our group dinner. I was relieved to see that both the man and the woman were in sync in such an honest way. This is all too rare.

The girl made it very clear to all of us that she had no interest in going on dates to try to get to know someone. Her approach was more logical—spend some time with him, hang out with his friends, and get to know him. Well, the cynical men wouldn't budge, and they kept giving her a hard time. I could tell she was getting a little uneasy, but she stuck to her guns. I was intrigued and I told her to do what she wanted to do and not to listen to the peanut gallery. If those fools wanted to think that she was doing this, that, and the other thing with her date, that was their problem and not hers. I reminded her that how she chose to date—or not date—was nobody else's decision but hers. She smiled and carried on with her nondate and had a great time.

Meeting young women like this, with such conviction and inner strength, is an inspiration to me. She knows who she is in life, carries that over to who she is on a date, and is not about to let anyone throw her off her game. Unfortunately, many of us are much stronger in private than out in public when our principles are tested.

Venturing into the adventurous world of dating, relationships, and marriage is a great way to put our money where our mouth is and see what we are made of. No matter how strong we are privately, I have noticed that many women get a massive case of stage fright on dates and in relationships. Why are we so afraid to don the powerful personal identities that we *all* have as women? In front of our mirrors, safely tucked into the limits of our comfort zone, where everything is theoretical, it's *so* easy to describe the woman we will become in our next relationship.

We kick ourselves in the butt for mistakes made in relationships past, and vow to be perfect next time around. Do any of these sound familiar? "I won't let anyone walk all over me ever again." "Next time I'll speak up when I know the relationship isn't working for me." "I need to have my own life outside the relationship." This is the same principle that also makes it *really* easy for us to be the best relationship counselors ever created when it comes to giving our friends relationship advice. "How could you have not seen that coming?" "Why didn't you speak up for yourself?" "Why do you lose your mind whenever you're around him?" A good test of how much we have learned from our past relationship mistakes is how often we keep repeating those same mistakes in future relationships. If we keep falling into the same traps over and over, how much are we really learning and growing as people?

It's not that I believe we get a sudden case of amnesia about all our past mistakes when faced with the prospect of making a new relationship work. But I have seen some women let their sense of self and strength of identity go flying out the window in the face of a shiny new potential Prince Charming. At the first sign of a prospective relationship, it is easy to forget all our promises to ourselves about how "next time it will be different," and slide right back into familiar self-destructive patterns, such as trying to test a relationship by not using common sense, not being honest, playing games, and not being straightforward.

Some of those patterns can be downright silly to everyone except the individuals involved. The fallout from these mistakes and self-destructive patterns can be costly. As a television judge, I have seen enough relationships established by these destructive patterns. In most of these cases the litigants (as I think is true for many of us) are perfectly willing to throw common sense out the window because of loneliness, dependency, desperation, or other emotions that should never be the motivation for a trip to the grocery store, let alone a relationship.

A perfect example of when dependency meets loneliness and its consequences is a case I presided over on *Cristina's Court*. As is so common today, a couple met on a dating Web site. After only one week of communicating, the young man asked his new Internet sweetheart to move in with him. While you are questioning this man's sanity (not to mention the girl's), let me add that he proposed to her six weeks later.

Now, I do not doubt that true love can happen that quickly. It is possible, just like anything is possible. But what concerned me was the fact that he clearly had behavioral and psychological problems. And despite this, the girl said yes to the proposal. By bringing the case to us, they allowed us to get a glimpse into their lives to find out what was really going on behind the scenes. It was like two strangers deciding to be together because one was lonely and the other eager and naive— *great* reasons to start a relationship.

In another case where stupidity, not even loneliness or desperation, overrode all semblance of common sense and logic, I found myself resolving a financial conflict between strangers. Actually, the litigants were boyfriend and girlfriend. They met, the sparks of attraction started flying, and within weeks they decided to move in together. Their total attraction to each other completely overrode common sense. They apparently thought that because the attraction was strong, the relationship would also be. Well, they were wrong. In the midst of this *Fantasy Island* episode starring two strangers playing the parts of boyfriend and girlfriend, she loaned him money. He did not pay her back, of course. Why should he, since she was basically a stranger? Thank God the law distinguishes between fantasy and reality. We brought them both back to reality and made them live up to their obligations and responsibilities. The lesson here: Chemistry can be deceptive.

These (and so many more cases I presided over) are all examples of couples who went into relationships wearing blindfolds. They chose to ignore their own self-destructive patterns, ignore common sense and the flashing red warning signs that could be seen from outer space. Someone was bound to get hurt in each situation, and that was exactly what happened.

Each woman has her own way of handling dating, courtship, and relationships. Each of us has made our own mistakes while on the road to everlasting love, emotional security, and true happiness. We have also learned our own lessons that have made us stronger, wiser, and better equipped to handle the emotional whirlwind of a relationship the next time around. It is time to identify the mistakes that we as women commonly make in relationships, as well as our natural strengths and advantages that we bring into each of our relationships. If we do this, dating and falling in love might actually become exciting instead of an exercise in self-doubt, confusion, and constant analysis. ("What is he thinking?" "What did he really mean by that?" "Is he thinking what I am?")

Dating and falling in love are supposed to be fun! Yet sometimes I get the feeling we are working so hard to make it fit into some ideal scenario we've created in our minds as to how the perfect relationship should unfold that we miss all the fun along the way. Going with the flow might be a little scary at times, like a roller coaster. But it also might be the most thrilling ride of your life *because* it is not entirely under your control. The best you can do is climb into the coaster, pull the safety bar down, take a deep breath, and go where the ride takes you.

But instead, many women's experience of dating and falling in love is a different fantasy. They have imagined it forever, *mapped out* all the details of their perfect man, how they will fall in love, how the courtship will play out, and every detail of the proposal and wedding, right down to the table centerpieces at the reception. Inevitably, life does not play out anything like you have planned, especially in relationships, where a whole other person is involved.

When women finally accept the fact that we cannot control every last detail of our relationships, most of us have the good sense to accept it, move forward, and enjoy the ride. Some women, however, make a less healthy choice. Unwilling to believe that they cannot completely control the relationship, they try to mold it and shape it into their fantasy.

Here is a perfect example from *Cristina's Court* of what happened when a woman tried to turn her fantasy relationship into reality. On the surface the case was about what happens when one person thinks she is loaning money and the other person thinks he is receiving a gift. What I have learned is that, one, there is simply not that much gift giving going on in the world, and two, that it is *never* just about the money in these relationship cases.

The plaintiff, a woman, desperately sought to buy her beloved's affection through loans, gifts, and other financial terms of endearment— not the smartest way to earn someone's love. The more she shelled out, the more her man criticized and berated her. The more she gave, desperately seeking his approval, the more he pulled away. Finally, the money ran out and so did he.

Why would a woman allow herself to get sucked into such a vicious cycle? She thought he was perfect, or at least she had convinced herself he was because she was so desperate. She wanted him at any cost. Listening to her story, I felt like she had always wanted the fantasy of having a man in her life. Like many women, she felt she needed someone to complete her, and she would do anything, at all costs, to get this ideal image of a man, even if that meant buying the man's affection. This is very dangerous, because in this case, she was exchanging her vision of Prince Charming for a cruel, demeaning man who sought to destroy her identity and her personality. The more she gave, the farther she drifted from being able to get out. She weakened who she was in her obsession with having a man at all costs.

Dating Strengths and Weaknesses

By the time we reach a certain age, it is impossible for us not to have figured out what we want. We have certainly had enough life experiences to figure out what is good for us and what is not so good, right? If we are smart and acknowledge our strengths and weaknesses, there is no reason on earth why we would not know what we want in life, or at least have a general idea.

There is nothing wrong with admitting to ourselves that we know what we want and even telling our partner. It may not be easy sometimes, and we certainly have a way of denying it, especially when challenged, but as women we know exactly what we want, what we expect, and what will ultimately make us happy.

Most of us have known what we wanted since we were old enough to be aware of the opposite sex, planned our wedding, and named our future kids. So why do we play the "I don't really know what I want; what do you want?" game so much?

Think about it: One of the reasons strong women are so attractive to the opposite sex is our self-confidence, strength of identity, and the power that we exert over our own lives. As I have been reiterating throughout the book, attitude is by far the sexiest hat a woman can wear. That is why your date, partner, or future husband was likely drawn to you in the first place.

Now, as soon as our new love asks us what we want out of life, they are suddenly supposed to believe us when we flutter our eyes, blush, and declare bashfully, "I don't know. Why don't you tell me? I'm okay with whatever you want." They are not stupid, and I guarantee they don't think we are either. Now they are desperately wondering why we are suddenly pretending our smart, sexy, successful brain just slid out of our smart, sexy, and successful head. Playing the "I don't know what I want; what do you want?" game only leads to confusion, miscommunication, and generally emotional muddiness, either now or later in the relationship.

Are we afraid that if we admit what we want and don't get it, the damage will be irreversible, or are we afraid of rejection? What do we think will actually happen if we tell a man how we feel and what we honestly want out of life, without censoring ourselves or saying what we think he wants to hear? Do we envision him jumping out of his seat, tossing a drink in our face, and saying, "Well, clearly you are a madwoman with crazy ideas about life that I not only do not share, but I find completely disturbing, and on top of that I think you are a nutcase, and I'm going to tell everyone I know about you."

Nobody's personal wish list for her life is strange enough to scare a man, especially if he is already at least mildly interested already. Men know what they want out of life, and all we have to do is ask if we want to find out. Men do not ask women what we want as a way of tricking us, cornering us, blackmailing us, or as some secret plot to emotionally destroy us. Men ask these questions because they honestly want to know and possibly see how well it lines up with what they want. This is not to judge or belittle women's ambitions either. When someone asks us what we want, we should find the courage to tell them. What is the worst thing that is going to happen? They're going to leave?

Besides, they are asking for a reason. Knowing what we want can be our greatest strength going into relationships, but if we don't have the courage to speak up, it can easily turn into our greatest weakness.

Now that we are addressing weaknesses, I probably don't even have to tell you our biggest dating downfall as women. You have probably already thought of it: overthinking. After all, as women we have a natural tendency to overthink situations to death without realizing it until it's too late and the damage has been done. We have the tendency to ascribe meaning where there is none. We just cannot accept that a situation is what it is without first examining and overanalyzing it from every possible angle, wearing our Agatha Christie sleuth caps, looking for evidence that we are somehow being tricked. We project our own assumptions, presumptions, and paranoid notions on the poor guy we are dating. Then, as if the whole situation is a science experiment, we carefully observe his reaction for confirmation that our suspicions (along with those of our girlfriends) were right all along.

Why can't we just accept the old adage that what you see is what you get? Accept that there may be a perfect man for each woman out there, but there is no such thing as a fantasy man. There is no perfect Prince Charming. However, this doesn't mean that we have to search for and even invent flaws and drama where there are none.

We all know that life is a struggle, and how that generally makes our achievements worth even more. However, as women we have somehow translated that concept into the idea that we need to struggle, and that when a struggle does not appear to exist, we should manufacture one just for good measure.

I saw on the television show *Sex and the City* a common example of how we women shoot ourselves in the foot while waiting for the other shoe to drop in a relationship. The main character, Carrie, had thoroughly convinced herself that the only single men left in New York were circus freaks, and that she had no chance of finding a normal guy to date. Of course, no sooner had she made that snap judgment of mankind than a normal guy asked her out. They began dating, and the more normal he seemed, the more suspicious Carrie became. Until finally, one morning when he left his apartment to go hang out with the guys, she ransacked his apartment, determined to find his freaky secret. She found nothing, but when he discovered her tearing apart his stuff, he declared *her* the freak and told her to hit the road. This still makes me laugh.

While most women do not go to the same paranoid extremes that television characters have the luxury to explore, we have our own real-world ways of handling situations that are too good to be true. We instantly become the guy's psychic, therapist, prophet, and private investigator (slap that Agatha Christie hat on again). We ask ourselves how this could possibly be so easy. We *need* to know why there isn't a struggle. We just have to find out what this perfect man is hiding and when the other shoe will finally and inevitably drop. We think about past relationships (the failed ones) and all the back-and-forth, the mind games, the guessing, the drama, the constant excitement of wondering how the guy really felt. None of that has happened in this one, so there must be something wrong, right?

This man has *no* idea of all this suspicion, self-doubt, paranoia, and assumption that is swirling around. In the man's mind, he has met a woman he really likes and is attracted to, and he's eager to find out where it goes. In your mind, his next phone call will be to tell you either that he's married, he wants to break up with you, or he has decided he doesn't want to be with women after all.

Now, here you are doing your best to decipher the *real* problem behind the relationship, but the man has no idea that he is an accidental costar in a theatrical drama, and in the meantime the relationship continues moving forward because you don't have the guts to speak up about your concerns. What happens next? You start playing games—another major dating downfall.

That's right, light the torch and release the doves—let the mind games begin. Dating is a battle where someone has to be conquered, and you're determined that it is not you. Since you are unwilling to be honest with yourself and with the man you're dating, you decide that the best course of action is to play mind games. You have now handed down the sentence, and it is his job to prove that he is not a cheating, emotionally disturbed serial killer out to destroy you emotionally.

So you also start playing hard-to-get. God forbid he thinks you need him, or even worse, that you like him. We've been there before, right? We have fallen in love too hard, too fast, and attached too quickly with expectations that were too high. This time will be different. You'll show him. Only which "him" are you punishing exactly? Are you taking revenge on all your old boyfriends, this new man, or the "him" looking in the mirror? I'm sure I don't have to tell you how unhealthy any kind of games are, how nobody ever wins (least of all you), and how all they do is get in the way of real life and, in the case of dating, your real chance at love and happiness.

Yes, life can be a struggle, but for goodness' sake, don't create a natural disaster when there's not even a hint of a cloud in the sky. If the sky is clear and the sun is out, don't do a rain dance. The best way to enjoy these experiences is to be smart and straightforward and enjoy the ride.

The final dating downfall occurs when that ride comes to a crashing halt with a broken heart. It is the instinct to choose revenge over moving on. It is some women's need to go down fighting when they feel scorned or abandoned, instead of just accepting the end of a relationship as just that—the end.

I heard a case on *Cristina's Court* of a couple who had dated for a while, had a reasonably good relationship, and even lived together. But apparently whatever attraction brought them together eventually wore off; the man started seeing someone else on the side and soon moved out. The man clearly did not have the same perception of how the breakup went as did the beautiful, professional, and extremely hurt and pissed-off woman whom he had left behind. He naively went on with his life, thinking of it as just another breakup.

A few months later the man was hit out of the blue from the state he lived in with a bill for over thirty-seven hundred dollars in unpaid tolls. The tolls were incurred from his toll-pay box that he would normally attach to the visor in his car, to be scanned as he drove on the state's toll roads. He was puzzled because he had not been using the toll box on the dates listed on the bills (which were now with collection agencies). In fact, he had not even been in town on those dates. Finally, he put two and two together and realized that the last time he had seen the toll box was in his ex-girlfriend's car. The man finally closed the book on this breakup by petitioning the state to send him photos of the person in the driver's seat when the toll box was scanned. Such photos are taken automatically as cars speed through the tollbooths. Sure enough, the driver in the photos was her.

She was having a great time, as it turned out, speeding along the state's tollways, with the meter ticking off those twenty-dollar fines time after time. She knew all the bills were being mailed directly to the toll-box owner (their old address where she still lived). This was a thirty-seven-hundred-dollar feel-good time for a woman scorned.

That is one example of how one woman cleverly (and not in a good way) harnessed some automated technology to exact revenge on an ex-boyfriend. As technology advances, so do the methods that other women are using to let the world know the messy details of their heartbreak.

Revenge, meet the latest and greatest technology in connecting with the world through a click of the mouse: social networking. The Internet has been used to help people find one another—and perhaps even plant the seeds of love—for some time now. Matchmaking Web sites and even Internet classified ads have served their purpose in introducing people who quite possibly would never have met otherwise. After all, it's a big world out there, and people are working harder than ever. Sometimes it is just unrealistic to think that you will meet that elusive right person for you at the neighborhood watering hole or through a blind date. If this is how you want to go about finding your mate, then all the power in the world to you (as long as you are careful and safe).

But now there is a new disturbing trend in cyberlove: airing one's dirty laundry for the whole World Wide Web to see. The newest way in which social networking Web sites are affecting people's relationships has nothing to do with creating new relationships and everything to do with how relationships are being ended and the often nasty aftermath. I will not delve into a Social Networking 101 technical manual of how people communicate on each of the many Web sites. Because believe me, I am *not* the person to teach that course! For the most part, I stick to the joys of e-mail and good old-fashioned telephone calls, and I couldn't be happier.

The gist of this new social networking trend is that there are quite a few brokenhearted souls out there who are not moving on. They are not gaining perspective or suffering through their grieving at the end of a relationship. They are going online for one reason and one reason alone—revenge. Once the relationship is over and someone has apparently been burned, the burn victim finds closure by communicating to the world, including all the couple's mutual friends, members of the community, family (ouch!), business contacts, and anyone else they can think of. They boldly announce what this person has done, from their point of view, and what they think of them. And from what I understand, it can get pretty nasty.

Did you just hear my loud sigh? This is a huge thing I disagree with, and I am embarrassed by my fellow women when they exact revenge this way—and any other way, Net or no Net. They are not humiliating the man; they are humiliating themselves. Knowing our strength as women, there is absolutely no reason to let ourselves be overcome by such immature tactics.

It also reminds me of the lengths that the public will go to, to dissect the same personal, often nasty details of celebrity breakups and divorce battles. I am continually mystified by the purpose of such a public airing of personal grievances.

And now it seems like the general public is imitating this tabloid mentality through social networking Web sites, e-mails, the Internet, and even the billboards that some women have been known to rent to announce to the world that they know their husband is cheating. Why would we possibly want to succumb to such humiliating behavior and cheapen ourselves?

It is hard to fully explain how passive-aggressive behavior like this gets under my skin and makes me wonder what people are thinking. First of all, exactly how interested are the neighbors in the nasty details of your breakup? Answer: not at all. Second, there is no *possible* benefit in engaging in this behavior. Revenge, cyber or otherwise, will not help you grieve the end of your relationship any quicker; it will only make the observers of your behavior think less of you, and if you have any kind of conscience at all, there will be a day when you regret your behavior.

In this situation, it may not be as difficult to forget what you have done. You have created a trail of evidence that links you to everyone who saw the results of your cyber-revenge that may last for much longer than you planned. It may even last into future relationships, when a future husband or even children can see how you chose to handle obstacles in life. The writing literally is on the wall about how you chose to handle the end of your relationship.

Moving In or Moving On

It happens every time: Whenever a new generation of young women comes along, bursting out of the gate full throttle into life with tons of awesome, free-spirited, and strong ideas about life, there are inevitably members of the previous generation who insist that everything is different for them in all aspects of their life than it was for women before them.

In some ways this is true, but not in the areas that matter most in life. For instance, I'll give the current generation their video games that sometimes make things look more real than they do in real life. They can also have their swollen texting thumbs from keeping everyone they know on all their social networking Web sites constantly updated about their every thought and move. Technology, music, fashion, and pop culture trends will always change. The way women and men meet has even changed since my husband and I met. That's all well and good, and to each her own.

Something that will never change, however, is what happens after that. There is a very genuine, heartfelt, and universal core to dating, courtship, and relationships that has been around for a long time, and I don't see it ever changing. I've noticed how the dating and relationship soap opera plays out the same for the young ladies who work in my office now as it did for my girlfriends and me back when we were their ages. Life is cyclical that way.

I watch how the dramas play out, and I have to laugh (and also groan and roll my eyes sometimes) as I watch those girls go through all the same things that I went through and make all the same mistakes I did, over and over again. I think to myself, *If I knew then what I know now, I could have avoided so many hours of unnecessary worrying and stressing out over what turned out to be such clear-cut situations with men.*

One of the biggest relationship questions I see women today struggling with is that of whether they should move in with a man out of wedlock. This issue was around back when I was dating, but the attitudes toward and acceptance of cohabitation have changed a bit since then. Recent studies are showing that fewer couples are choosing to get married these days but still choosing to live together as an alternative.

I personally do not believe in living with someone before you get married. Call me traditional, old-fashioned, or anything else that you associate with this statement, but for me (emphasis on the word *me*), it is just not right and never has been.

My husband and I dated for over six years before we got married, and never once did we contemplate any kind of free trial period of cohabitation. I had no intention of cooking, cleaning, doing laundry, and playing house for a man I was not even married to. The fact that my parents would kick my booty if I moved in with a man outside of marriage also had a lot to do with it. In all seriousness, my decision not to cohabit was based on my own personal and family values about marriage, and yours should be too. I understand that many women see the decision to live with their boyfriend before considering marriage as a way of decreasing the risk and liability of a big step like marriage. Interestingly enough, studies show that divorce rates have basically remained unchanged since this line of reasoning first started becoming popular.

But if you believe cohabitation is right for you because you (or your partner) are trying to avoid the legal complications of marriage, I am going to have to burst your bubble. The legal and financial consequences of cohabiting can be just as bad as, if not worse than, those of marriage. The reason that it is even more dangerous to cohabit is because there is no legal, binding contract (i.e., marriage certificate) governing what happens if you split up—from deciding ownership of that big-screen television you bought together to, more important, the baby you had together. The custody issues surrounding a baby born out of wedlock are legally messy and just as, if not more, emotionally trying than custody cases between married people, not to mention enormously unfair to the child.

Now—and certainly not to compare the two issues—let's move on to that big-screen television. Say that he puts it on his credit card and you give him money for it. If the two of you break up, there is no way to prove that you gave him that money. It is your word against his, and those of you who have seen *Cristina's Court* have seen how many of these formerly cohabiting couples managed to become litigants on the show.

One case that I am reminded of was about a cohabiting unmarried couple who taught everyone in the courtroom that day how to turn sponging gifts into an art form. The woman in the case worked and worked and worked to earn a good living. She was definitely the breadwinner of the household, and her boyfriend quickly took note of this. He also saw her as Santa Claus and made his list of toys: truck, boat, Harley-Davidson—all things that "they" needed. She bought these things for him, and he eventually sponged her out of everything she had, and then, when the relationship inevitably ended, she sued him for the return of all the things. She tried to get them all back. We looked closely at her intentions, actions, words, and based on those things, the items were all labeled as gifts that she had voluntarily bought for him.

This is exactly why it is dangerous when you buy things for somebody else—especially expensive things within the fuzzy boundaries of cohabitation. It is hard to later prove whether those things are a gift or a loan. If this couple had been married and had bought these things with joint money, they could have legally divided the items or agreed to sell them and split the profits or agree who would take what.

In addition to the legal and financial issues of cohabitation, an equally important issue to examine while making this decision is the expectations you and your partner have. Are you agreeing to live with this man because in the back of your mind, in a place you would never admit to him (and barely yourself), you believe it will lead to marriage? That kind of thinking can easily backfire in the future and have very messy consequences. Never do anything in your relationship, including making life-altering decisions such as cohabitation, based on assumptions or secret expectations. It is not fair to the other person, and it's certainly not fair to your emotional well-being. Gather up your courage, confront your partner, and make absolutely sure that you both are on the same page in terms of life goals, personal values, and plans before you move in.

When I hear of women agreeing to move in while secretly expecting a marriage proposal, it makes me wonder if women are changing what they really want or if they're just settling for the best deal they think they can get. Are women exchanging an engagement ring for a house key? Settling for less can be very dangerous to your identity, and it seems to be a recent trend among women.

Statistically speaking, *most* women of past generations wanted to get married, have kids, and live out the whole "picket fence and a dog" scenario. What's the matter with that? This does not make women less liberated and powerful if this is what they want and they're not afraid to say it. Absolutely not. In fact, it's the opposite. By expressing what they want with certainty, rolling the dice, and taking the chance that the man they are dating may or may not want the same thing, these women are being true to themselves. Do not be afraid to speak up and ask the questions in your heart. But most important, don't be afraid to hear the answer.

However, today, with the increasing number of women now choosing cohabitation in lieu of marriage, I fear that there are some negotiators in our midst. I fear that many women are compromising their values and denying to themselves what they actually want or, as I just mentioned, hoping against all realistic expectations that their man will suddenly see the light and pop the question.

Do you see why the picket-fence women are so strong? They know what they want and they are not afraid to ask for it. If they are dating a guy and suddenly find out he is headed down a completely different road than they are, their verdict is crystal clear: *Hit the road, Jack!* They know what they want and they refuse to compromise in getting it. Men will appreciate this kind of honesty in relationships.

Like those women, men too know exactly what they want. They may not feel the need to tell you until they are good and ready, but they will eventually tell you. Unfortunately it may come about very suddenly and in the form of a breakup if they feel pressure to do something that they *don't* want to do (like get married if all they wanted to do was live together). When the time and circumstances are right, men have no problem telling you exactly what they want and don't want. They will most often try to spare your feelings if they know for a fact that what they want doesn't align with what you want. This may be upsetting to them, but in their minds, the world will continue spinning on its axis, life will go on, and they will figure you just were not the one for them. This is why it is important to have the value-alignment conversation much sooner than later. And by later, I mean when you're having the duplicate key made, cordoning off closet space, and assigning him a parking spot.

Don't Go Wasting Your Emotions

Despite our best intentions, efforts, honesty, negotiations, and the strong feelings we have for the other person, the fact is that many relationships were simply never meant to be and they end. Statistically speaking, you will be in a whole lot more unsuccessful relationships than successful ones. Since this can be a rather depressing way of looking at it, think of it this way: You have to kiss a lot of frogs before you find your prince (as the fairy tale goes). The problems that occur are for the women who get stuck on the frogs, waste their time and emotions, and forget to keep moving forward in their search for the prince. Reality check: If the relationship was meant to be you would still be in it.

Yet I have seen many women deny this over and over. They often hang on to the foolish notion that although the relationship has ended, this man really, secretly is perfect for them, and if she is patient, he will eventually come back to her. This is a selfish way of thinking that attempts to rob the man of his free will and robs you of your time, energy, and potential happiness in all your future relationships. Women get stuck in past relationships that they feel are somehow unresolved, and they feel compelled to hang on (this is in their mind—not the man's). They believe that if the stars align just right and the man gets hit on the head just hard enough, he may come to his senses and return on bended knee with a ring. This kind of thinking breaks my heart to see, especially in my friends and loved ones, because I watch as they prevent themselves from giving any of their future relationships a chance. An entire piece of their heart is still hung up on this fantasy notion of their perfect man finally returning. There is a shadow of the past looming over any chance they have of finding love.

Things get even more complicated in these on-again, off-again relationships during which, sometimes over an extended period of time, the same couple stays locked in an endless circle of breaking up and reuniting. In a way this is like watching a dog chase its tail. Clearly, one or both partners in the relationship do not know what they want, yet they are too stuck in the idea that somehow if they give it just one more shot, it may be different. Or maybe they hang on simply because it is convenient and safe. How can this be if neither person is apparently learning anything about him- or herself or the relationship, and yet they think the relationship will fix itself? Relationships cannot fix themselves any more than if you leave your broken-down car in the driveway overnight and hope it will miraculously start the next morning.

The on-again, off-again relationship is also harmful because, in most situations, the man and woman are participating in this endless cycle for two entirely different reasons. The woman may secretly be rationalizing that if he didn't really love her he would not keep coming back over and over. She may believe in the innermost part of her soul that the next time he comes back it will be for good and possibly include an engagement ring.

Big reality check: In these situations, the man may be settling for the best he can get until something better comes along (whether he will ever admit this or not). While there is nothing wrong with wanting to find the best person, it is very unfortunate that some men (and some women) have the habit of stringing along "second-best" while continuing their search. As much as we scream and yell at how unfair this is, it is our job as smart, empowered women to be aware of this and find the strength to break the cycle. Unfortunately, the way these fiascos *usually* end is with the man finally finding that elusive woman who he feels is the best fit for him, and breaking the heart of the on-again, off-again woman. And if you think about it, it really is not all his fault.

This entire cycle and resulting heartbreak could easily be avoided if women would be honest with themselves and with their partners. Resolve *not* to allow yourself to be blindly led into the on-again, off-again cycle, because in your heart you know exactly where it may be headed. Remember, it takes two to tango. Life is too short to waste time playing these endless games.

Do not go wasting your emotions on a man (or a relationship) who is on an entirely different page of the relationship than you are, is clearly not the one you are meant to be with, and is absolutely not wasting his emotions crying about the relationship and the subsequent breakup like you are. When a breakup happens, do not go into victim mode. Yes, it is okay to take some time to mourn the loss of this person who was special to you, whom you shared good times with, and whom you had a connection with.

But the danger comes when you remain paralyzed in that place where emotions override common sense and rational thinking. There you are, moping around, crying, "Woe is me," and contemplating your newly formed identity as damaged goods that no man wants to be around. What do you think he is doing? I guarantee it has nothing to do with moping, and he *certainly* is not taking these self-deprecating shots to his identity that you are.

The breakup of one relationship (or even many) is not a reflection on the identities of the people involved. You are still the same person you were before this relationship, regardless of the breakup. A breakup is not a hit to your identity, and therefore beating yourself up and needlessly wasting your emotions on it is downright ridiculous.

Breakups are such an organic part of nature. Just as snakes molt and shed their skin, people move on from relationships that have naturally played themselves out. Unlike many people, snakes have a healthy way of moving on: After shedding their skins they never look back. And why shouldn't they do this? They don't need it. However, as humans (albeit with much bigger brains for emotions to swirl around in), we need closure. As women in particular, we need ten million different explanations as to why a relationship ended. We need an answer and we need it *now*.

This kind of thinking is all well and good if you are a crime scene investigator, except that the end of a relationship does not constitute an actual crime. Nobody did anything wrong here, including you and—as much as you would like to place blame—your ex-boyfriend. So put away the crime scene chalk and fingerprinting kit. It simply did not work out. Move on.

Even if you did get that elusive answer you are seeking, will that be enough? Of course not—you will always want more. You think the breakup is because of something you did or a personal flaw that you can fix for your next relationship. I am all about self-awareness and self-development, but in this case you are beating yourself up for no reason. He did not reject *you* as a human being—he rejected having a relationship with you. And if you are being honest with yourself and looking at the relationship objectively, you will probably see the same problems with the relationship that he did. And if not, let it go anyway.

A partnership that you happened to be one member of has been dissolved, through no fault of either party. Just because the identity of the relationship was flawed does not mean that your identity is flawed too. You will never likely find that external closure you are looking for. Sometimes in life, we just need to make the conscious decision to make peace with a situation and move on. If you do not move on, if you get stuck and waste emotions on something that was not meant to be, there is a good chance you will miss the right person when they do come along.

Looking back on my own dating life and observing the dating habits of young women I know, I realize how much perspective I have gained just by getting older and wiser, and putting breakups into perspective.

I think of my first real breakup quite a bit. Not because I have any lingering regrets from the relationship, but rather because of what I learned from it. He was my first serious long-term relationship and my first love. I remember being so consumed by the relationship. I made him my everything. It was wonderful for that time in my life, perhaps because the insecurity of having just entered college made me so vulnerable in all other areas of my life that I was looking for something safe and familiar. I wanted the relationship to work so that at least one area was constant and the same.

But even in the midst of all this perceived security, I realized with my infamous woman's sixth sense that the relationship was over. Yet I was too young to know that it was my sixth sense telling me this. Nevertheless, I instinctively knew that you cannot force a relationship in the way that I was forcing this one. That is how you know it is the wrong relationship. I knew in my heart that he was not the guy for me, but I kept hanging on and denying this.

Meanwhile, this poor guy was politely hanging in there, trying to slowly break up with me, and I was not helping the situation *at all.* It all came to a head, my denial and this guy trying to rip the Band-Aid off, when we were at a sorority dance. I was in the midst of telling him how happy I was he was in my life and how much I loved (at least I thought I did) and cared for him. That was the exact moment when he broke up with me. Looking back now, I can laugh, and I certainly have no hard feelings toward the guy. But I felt stupid and ridiculous sitting there, deep in denial, while trying to force something that so clearly was not meant to be, to the point where I was showering him with all this dependent affection. Even today when I think about it, it makes me feel a little sick.

At the time, however, I was devastated. But at the same time I knew it—I had no doubt that this was not the relationship for me. I felt all along that the breakup was imminent. I kicked myself for not knowing what I knew. You always remember lessons like that. That breakup taught me my most valuable dating lesson: Listen to your heart, listen to yourself, and listen to your partner, and you will know when feelings are reciprocal.

I have found that if you do not know what it is like to meet the right person—when those feelings of love are reciprocal—you try to make everyone the right person. The right dating experience or relationship should not feel like a constant challenge—like you are constantly forcing it to work or pushing against the very rules of nature. If that is the relationship you are in, most likely you have not yet met the right person for you.

All I can tell you is that the real right person will come along, usually when you least expect it. I realize this can be very frustrating for single people to hear. But let me assure you that I know many women who have found the right person and, much to their own surprise, have found this to be frighteningly true. Nobody has a crystal ball. Sometimes you have to take risks, but you just have to trust that it will happen.

Ironically, as I write this book my daughter's favorite movie (and song) is *Mamma Mia!*, and in all her childhood innocence, her favorite song from the movie is called "Lay All Your Love on Me." Fittingly enough, when I was listening to the lyrics of this song they reminded me of this particular dating law.

As you navigate through the inevitable maze of breakups, for all the women out there who continually waste their emotions on the wrong person, this song is for you: "Don't go wasting your emotion . . . Don't go sharing your devotion . . . Lay all your love on me." "Me" refers to the person who really deserves it.

My Verdict

Dating is an unpredictable journey that never follows the script from your fantasies. Nevertheless, throughout the trials and tribulations of finding the man that is perfect for you, remember this: A strong woman has faith in herself.

"IN HER OWN WORDS"

I asked some smart, confident women to share their thoughts on the laws covered in this chapter. Here is what they said along with my responses.

What strengths do we bring into dating?

1. "As women we can heal broken hearts, but at the same time turn around and be heartbreakers, and then love the wrong person for us—sometimes all at the same time."

CP: I think we are so eager to find a partner that at times we forget to just enjoy life.

Why do you think women often let our emotions get the best of us?

Continued

1. "We are, by nature, emotional creatures who think with our hearts. We have to because we are the caring, nurturing ones. It isn't always healthy, but I think it's just what makes us women!"

CP: I love this because she doesn't make any excuses. She recognizes and embraces the inherent identity of a woman. We should be proud to be caring and nurturing.

2. "I feel like my emotions keep me in check and tell me what's right or wrong in my life. When I am upset it does take a while for that pain to heal, but I see that as a reminder not to let myself get into such a situation again in the future."

CP: This is a great example of the power of a woman's sixth sense. We all have it; we just need to start paying attention to it.

3. "The smartest women in the world sometimes do things that are entirely based on emotion and are completely irrational. For instance, logically I should not want to carry a child inside my body for nearly ten months; spend hours in agony, painfully pushing said child out of my body; and then be sleep-, food-, and sunlight-deprived for months afterward. Emotionally, though, I've never wanted anything as much as I wanted that experience. Life would be completely boring without emotion. We may as well be a nation of robots."

CP: Women are masochists! We love torture. Only we can take something so painful like childbirth and turn it into a beautiful experience. Why? Because we're the only ones who can do it.

4. "I don't consider myself an emotional person. My doctor didn't believe me when I was in labor because apparently I wasn't acting hysterical enough. But internally I do take things

very personally when things don't go right or if I make a mistake, particularly if it will impact others."

CP: This shows how every woman expresses emotion in a different way. This woman is strong because she knows this about herself. You can't judge the way you react to life.

What are the best lessons you have learned from dating?

1. "I learned to put myself first. I also learned that no matter what I do wrong it never means I deserved abuse."

CP: I admire this woman's strength. It shows that if you do not have a self-worth to defend, dating will be a nightmare: a rollercoaster ride where people will chip at whatever self-worth you have.

2. "It's always better to be honest than try to lie your way through a relationship. Even though the truth hurts sometimes, it's better to be aware of issues so they can be worked on."

CP: We should never try to push our way through a relationship that is not meant to be. Our woman's sixth sense will tell us this.

3. "I have learned that my time with different people may not last forever, but when they go it is not because they no longer love me or never loved me. It is nothing about me or faults of my own. It's simply that our time is up and our paths have diverged."

CP: This is a great point. The only people we own are ourselves. This makes us aware that we are responsible only for ourselves. That is why relationships are made up of two people. You cannot control fate.

CHAPTER 5

Law #5: *Understand the Rules of Engagement*

My husband and I dated for over six years before we got married. We dated as law school students and through our first years of grunt work as lawyers. But let's face it: Even as a young, frantically busy career woman and lawyer working her way up in the industry, I did not forget how to read a calendar. After six years of birthdays, Christmases, New Year's Eves, and lots of dates, I started to wonder, *Where is this going? What do I want? What does he want?*

There was only one way to find out. I confronted him. I was not angry, bitter, or manipulative, and I certainly didn't threaten him or give him an ultimatum. All I wanted to know was what he wanted. It really was that simple. I was not looking for a marriage proposal or anything like that. But I did want to find out where our relationship was going and if we were on the same page in terms of what we wanted for our future. I wanted to make sure that our decision to invest so much in this relationship was a good one, and one that aligned with our personal values and what we both wanted out of life. My thinking was that if he didn't love me the way I thought I loved him, then that was my problem and I would have to deal with it on my own. I knew we were committed to each other, but I didn't know if we loved each other. Were we putting the opinions of others in our lives ahead of our own, without being true to ourselves?

I call this *relationship by committee.* I created the term to describe the tendency that we as women have to gather the full tribunal of women in our lives to make decisions as a group as to how to proceed with the relationship. You know what I'm talking about. When you first start dating someone, everything your new "intended" says and does is the subject of intense speculation and scrutiny. "If he said that he means this, you know." "If he does that then he's thinking that." And later, "Girlfriend, you know he's thinking this about you, so you'd better either dump him or give him an ultimatum! Don't let him get away with this!"

I will not delve too deeply here into all the obvious relationship complications such ganging-up behavior can cause. But I will say this: Letting other people's opinions dictate and complicate anything in our lives, especially the most important things, like relationships, family, and career matters, is disrespectful to our relationships and disrespectful to our individual identities.

To ensure that this was not the case, I approached Christopher for a frank and honest conversation about our relationship. I was direct in sharing all my concerns with him. When I paused to give him a chance to respond, to reassure me, to contradict me, to tell me he loved me, to tell me I was crazy—anything—all I got in return was silence. Finally, he said, "I have no idea." And then he was silent again.

I was absolutely brokenhearted. His deafening silence was the most devastating reaction I could never have imagined going into that conversation. I really adored him, but as hard as it was for me, I broke up with Christopher, my crazy Nuyorican who would later become my husband. It was only fair to me and him. Yes, there are challenges like this, but if we have the strength of identity to get real with ourselves and the other person and be straightforward about our intentions, we can overcome those challenges. Looking back, I learned that sometimes we have to risk it all to gain something greater.

Within a few days of the breakup he called and proceeded to tell me everything he thought I wanted to hear—that he loved me, needed me, and would do whatever it took to make me happy. For many women that would have been the end of it, game, set, and match. But I knew better. He was suddenly acting weak and was not the self-assured guy I knew. Something was off.

Like I said, I knew Christopher better, and the agreeable person on the phone, giving me everything he thought I wanted, was not the man I knew. I instantly went into lawyer mode and cross-examined him until he finally admitted what I already knew from the beginning of the conversation—he didn't know much more than he did a few days before that. I told him we needed to spend time apart and think about where we were and what we each wanted. I was even more brokenhearted.

Christopher did not call again, but he did write a letter, months later, that answered all my questions. He explained how he felt about me. The only thing holding him back from expressing his true feelings before was fear. He was so afraid of commitment. This was also coupled with a crazy notion that he was not yet in a position to provide a stable financial life for me. He had just graduated from law school and was still looking for a job. To Christopher, admitting that he really loved me was the same as assuring that he could provide for me.

The honest, open conversation that followed about that letter and about our true feelings for each other gave me peace of mind and a renewed sense of optimism and clarity about our relationship. In order for any of this to happen, I had to be secure enough with myself and what I wanted to be willing to fold my cards and leave the table without looking back, good or bad. This is not just because Christopher told me what I wanted to hear or that our story had a happy ending. This is because I sought the clarity I needed about our relationship and didn't let fear stop me from telling the man I love what I wanted. I trusted myself enough to know that we had to figure out what was right for both of us, individually and as a couple.

The lesson I learned was not to be afraid to speak up and confront the hard questions in your relationship. This will bring you to a new level of honesty while strengthening your identity both as partners in the relationship and as individuals. There is nothing stronger, smarter, and sexier than confronting what you want, being who you are, and owning it with every ounce of your identity.

Rules of Engagement

When should you have a discussion with your longtime partner about getting married? Instead of making it a "to marry or not to marry" conversation, have an honest discussion with your partner about what the relationship means to both of you and where you see it going. Framing it as an honest, open-ended conversation, rather than as a yes-or-no question, will make you both confront what you want and find out if it's the same thing.

However, let's say your honest relationship discussion does come around to the question of marriage and whether you and your partner are ready to get engaged. How do you know if you are ready? We have all probably heard the marriage experts assign various amounts of time to this question. How do they know the perfect amount of time that each individual couple needs to make such an important life decision? Sociology studies, research, and statistics are informative and can certainly generate some very interesting conversations within relationships. But how much should they play into your personal decision? Not a lot.

The marriage decision is solely up to you and your partner. Remember that one of the morals behind all of my own laws is for you to exercise your strength of conviction and stop checking in with the committee for every life decision. By committee, remember that I mean everyone from family to friends, and even larger groups like church or society. In no way am I asking you to disrespect the good intentions and opinions of any of the groups I just listed. It is just that the opinions of outside parties should not affect your life decisions unless they reflect your own personal values.

But what happens when you and your partner do not agree on the answer to the marriage question? If your partner does not believe in marriage but still wants to be with you, should you stay or should you go? You need to decide for yourself, based on what you want in your heart, if this is a deal breaker for you. This is not an easy decision to make or an easy conclusion to come to. Believe me, I know this is hard. As I mentioned in the section on living together, this is a personal question based on your own personal values that you have to ask yourself and be *honest* with yourself about. If you are ever going to be in denial about anything with yourself, this is not one of those times.

Here is a compelling example of what happens when a woman is in denial with herself about what she wants versus what is actually being offered to her. Once again, from my bench on *Cristina's Court*, I was presented with a case that claimed to be about a loan repayment gone sour. Raise your hand if you think that's what the case was really about. You're right: It was not.

The female plaintiff wanted to marry her boyfriend. He did not want to get married to her or any other woman. He wanted to keep life simple, clean pools, live alone in his bachelor shack, and play cards with his buddies. She kept insisting on getting married. He kept saying he didn't want to get married. From their very first date, anyone paying attention would have seen that all this guy wanted to do was to enjoy his uncomplicated life. He would have made a great drinking buddy for Cliff and Norm on *Cheers*. Anyway, it was obvious to me and everyone else watching that if she wanted to walk down the aisle, she would be waiting a long time. But someone was not paying attention. Someone was not being honest with herself.

Talking him into it was not working, so she did the next logical thing (in her mind): She loaned him money. In a way, she was doing this to solidify a bond where there was none. She knew he could not repay her, but she decided to use the law, a binding contract, to seal the deal and trap him into a relationship with her.

After we got to know this woman, we realized that she was really smart—or so she thought. She thought she had it all figured out. Unfortunately for her, the law is not set up to be used for spite or, in her case, personal gain. In fact, I have observed from the bench that whenever people try to use the law for personal gain, revenge, or any other function that it is not intended for, it almost always backfires on them. The same is true when people try to use the law as a relationship fixer-upper, as a way of fixing their personal problems, or as their own personal ATM machine for some fast cash. The woman in this case was trying to use a financial contract to create a relationship one.

When you think about it, a breach of contract is the same as the breakup of a relationship. Contracts are broken every day, and so are relationships. Believing that a contract would hold up better than a relationship was the major flaw in her otherwise well-thought-out plan.

Women will eventually learn that money does not qualify as a loving term of endearment. I only hope I am still around to see this day. Well, as we can all conclude, he did not pay her back, and she sued him for the money. She was really exacting her revenge on him for not marrying her, and in a way she was trying to hold on. This was exactly what she wanted: a connection. I wonder if this woman is out there, still single and bankrupt.

Speaking of making mistakes, it pains me to have to address this next point—the ultimatum. It saddens me as a woman that this behavior even exists. What if your love just will not marry you (or do whatever it is you are asking of him), and you are unwilling to walk out the door and move on? An ultimatum is threatening, bullying, and disrespecting the man you are supposedly in love with in order to get something you want. Whether it is a marriage proposal or some other sort of commitment, I can barely fathom a woman saying to the love of her life, "It's my way or the highway." The ultimatum can come in the form of a deadline for the woman getting what she wants ("If I don't get a ring within the year I'm out of here"), or sometimes the woman will just continuously threaten to end the relationship until the man gives in.

This relationship power play can come from the woman's fear of abandonment, insecurity with herself and her place in the relationship, or an overwhelming urge to control another human being. Honestly, it really does not matter which specific reason it is. How can you justify telling another person that you disrespect him so much and care so little about what he wants that you are willing to threaten him to get what you want? This strategy is not good for you. Now think of the "do unto others" golden rule, and how it applies to this situation. Think about how you would feel if someone gave you an ultimatum instead of respecting who you are and what you want.

Now imagine if you actually do go through with a marriage ultimatum, even if it is against your better judgment. The man that you love goes along with it, surely against his own better judgment, and agrees to marry you. In your mind, you have won. You are the victor because you got what you wanted. Congratulations. But before you pop open the champagne and declare yourself queen for the day, there is something you need to think long and hard about: For the rest of your life, or however long your marriage lasts, there will be a question burning a hole in the back of your head (or at least there should be). Did he marry you because he loves you and wanted to marry you, or did he do it because of the ultimatum? As much as you try to convince yourself that he probably would have eventually proposed, ultimatum or not, you will never be sure. Can you be certain enough to look this man in the eye every day for the rest of your life without a single ounce of doubt? This is not a good foundation for any marriage.

Here is another pattern that we have seen when it comes to men and marriage, because we've seen it time and time again. You know all the men out there who have dated the same woman forever and ever and ever. The relationship does not seem to be going anywhere, and if the woman would just be honest with herself she would realize it too. For year after year, the woman hangs in there, and in some tragic cases even bears this man's children in hopes of a more permanent relationship (i.e., marriage). She waits and waits, just on the off chance that he may decide to marry her.

But even as she is hanging in there, getting more and more frustrated, she does not say a word, stagnating until she finally wills herself to exclaim, "Are we getting married or what?" I'm telling you, this can happen after one year, five years, or ten, but the outcome is uncannily similar.

With as much sincerity as he can muster, the man painstakingly explains to the woman that marriage is just not for him. Regardless of the reason he gives (past divorce, scars from previous relationships, he grew up in a broken home, etc.), the woman buys it and makes the decision to break up with him. She is at peace with herself for being honest and stating in no uncertain terms that she wants to be married. Good for her! She is happy with her decision, knowing in her heart that because he did not want to get married, he obviously wasn't the man for her. It's time to move on, find the right man, and live happily ever after, right? Not so fast. She hears it from mutual friends, acquaintances, colleagues, or the wedding announcements in the newspaper: Mr. I-don't-believe-in-marriage has tied the knot—and quickly.

Define *quickly* however you like, because no matter how much actual time has passed between the breakup and his impending nuptials, it seems like he was down on one knee proposing to another woman five minutes after breaking up with you. I can sympathize with women in this situation. This is a tough one to swallow. No matter how at peace you were with the breakup when it happened, this is a difficult thing to hear without completely losing your cool. How do you react?

Well, honestly, the blame rests on both of you. You failed to speak up sooner about your true feelings (as is one of our downfalls), and now he is looking for a way out. This is like a tandem parachute jump where someone has to pull the rip cord, nobody does, and everyone goes crashing into the ground together.

Even if you track this guy down, tie him to a chair, shine a bright light in his eyes, and interrogate him for hours, you will not get the satisfactory answer you're looking for. What is it that this guy can possibly tell you that will make you sleep better at night? Do you think he lied to you about not wanting to be married? I don't believe that is the case. In these situations, when he is sitting across from you discussing marriage, the man honestly believes that it is not an institution that is right for him at that time.

The truth of the situation is that he does not want to marry *you.* Besides, whether he does not want to get married at all or does not want to marry you—there is no difference as far as your life is concerned. This is not your fault, and I sincerely hope you believe that. Punishing him won't make you feel better, and neither will punishing yourself. He is not the man who is supposed to be your husband. Your woman's sixth sense is probably already telling you this. Do not ignore this. Admit that you know what you know.

Questions to Ask Before Marriage

Let's end our discussion about the rules of engagement on a much brighter note and discuss how to proceed toward marriage once you *do* find the man who is supposed to be your husband. Once you do find the person who you believe is right for you, there are some steps you can take to strengthen the foundation of your marriage before you even make it to the altar.

This mindfulness and reflection prior to marriage should be practiced by all engaged couples. Before my husband and I were married, for instance, we met with our church priest, Father Alden Sison, for our prewedding interview. Like good Catholics, we both expected a solemn lecture on the responsibilities that come with marriage and a thorough grilling on our intentions going into the bond of holy matrimony. After all, marriage is not an institution to be entered into casually, and a representative of the church is in an excellent position to issue this reminder to the newly engaged. However, Father Alden had just one question for us: "How long have your parents been married?" We told him that both sets of our parents had been married for over thirty-five years. Much to our surprise, that was the end of the prewedding interview.

Father Alden explained that because Christopher and I had spent a lifetime observing our parents maintaining their marital bonds, through good times and bad, we already had a solid understanding of marriage. He told us that we clearly knew how sacred marriage is, and gave us his blessing to move forward. Thinking back on that meeting I realize that Father Alden was right: I knew what marriage was going to be because I had watched my parents maintain their successful marriage for my entire life. After that meeting, neither Christopher nor I had any doubts that we were ready to be married.

I realize that many couples are not comfortable, for one reason or another, with looking to the church for premarital counseling. Some may choose premarital counseling with a therapist to explore their feelings about marriage and make sure that each partner is ready to walk down the aisle. There, under the supervision of a trained marriage counselor, they ask themselves and each other the honest questions that will either strengthen their bond going forward or, in worst-case scenarios, alert them to the fact that they may be jumping into marriage before they are ready.

Other couples may choose to explore these questions on their own, in an honest, open, forthright, and private conversation with each other. If you do, start by asking each other, "How do you see our marriage?" This creates an opportunity to discuss what you each admire about your parents' marriage, what mistakes you would like to avoid, concerns that either of you may have stemming from observing divorce within your family or among your friends, and how you see things changing after you each say, "I do." Even if neither of you sees things changing at all, it is an excellent question to get the conversation started and get you both thinking about the institution of marriage. Marriage is not, after all, a version of serious dating with matching rings.

Next, ask your partner if his expectations of you and your role in the relationship will likely change after the wedding. This is your chance to find out how your future spouse sees his role and identity as a married person versus a single one. Your future spouse may also be nervous that you may somehow change as a married woman versus as a single girl.

This is a valid point. I have seen how men talk to one another about us. I have overheard conversations about wives transforming from smart, self-confident, and sexy divas into homely, meek, frumpy women who intellectually and physically stop taking care of themselves and don't give their radical transformation a second thought.

There is a reason your partner became attracted to you in the first place, and vice versa. If he did not find you sexy or desirable in one way or another, you would be platonic friends, not man and wife. The attraction is what keeps your relationship feisty, and it is unfair to rob your partner of that part of you just because you get married. Yes, there are many other aspects of your identity that are not physical and that your husband undoubtedly is drawn to. This does not mean that it's okay to dismiss the whole package of who you are.

You can get married, have kids, and become a stay-at-home mom while still staying connected to the sexy piece of your identity and staying plugged into all the things you were interested in and passionate about when you were single. You do not have to lose yourself in the marriage.

The reason that many single men may wonder about this (either in their heads or out loud to women in the case of the braver ones) is because they fear the loss of any aspect of what attracted them to their partner in the first place. They are human and understand that people change over time, physically and otherwise. However, this premarriage fear is their way of expressing how attracted they are to your sexy, smart, and self-confident identity. This is why they may ask you questions like this.

There are no silly questions or answers in the engagement conversation, because what you are doing is defining your future identity as a married couple. It is much better to ask these questions of each other now than during the honeymoon, when the "till death do us part" reality sets in. Marriage is a joyous and positively life-changing event, and it is certainly not always easy. But it is also a serious step, and one that you and your partner should be fully prepared for.

My Verdict

Before engaging your heart, be sure that your head is already in gear. Know what you know, do not deny the obvious, and realize that when you say, "I do"—it's for real.

"IN HER OWN WORDS"

I asked some smart, confident women to share their thoughts on the laws covered in this chapter. Here is what they said, along with my responses.

What are the most important things a couple should find out about each other when getting engaged or considering marriage?

1. "Are you a junk collector? Do you stop and pick stuff up from the side of the road just because it is free? Are you a messy person? How often do you take a vacation from work but spend it working? Do you have a budget or do you spend each paycheck?"

CP: The first responses are the little quirks you find out about someone, similar to, "Are you sloppy or neat, and do you leave your underwear on the floor?" That's all well and good, but are these the most important things you need to learn about the person you aspire to spend the rest of your life with? Find out what their core principles are in life—their morals, how they feel about family, children, and friendship. When you meet someone and see how he feels about these things, it will really tell you what kind of person he is.

2. "Do you truly believe in 'for better or for worse'?"

CP: This is one of the most important things we have to know about the other person. This is also a great question, because "for better or worse" can mean different things to different people.

3. "Make sure you're on the same page about the big three things: money management, religion (not that you have to

Continued

be the same religion, just that you need to be able to live with your partner's views), and whether you both desire children or not."

CP: These *are* the three big things to learn about your partner. These are not topics to broach when you first meet, but after a few dates these are questions to start thinking about.

Should the goal of getting engaged be a priority when you start a relationship?

1. "Yes. I want to get married, and I'm at an age where I can't waste time on 'seeing where things go.' If I feel like a relationship can't transcend to a serious level, or if a guy tells me he doesn't believe in marriage, then I do move on, even if I have strong feelings for him. I know what I want and can't compromise that."

CP: That's a great answer if you're at the stage of your life and relationship where you feel that strongly about it. This is a healthy attitude to have, and many women don't have such clear-cut goals, so I admire this woman's clarity. But keep in mind that this is not subject material for the first date. Even if you think you know on the first date that this is the person for you, there is a right time and right place to communicate that, and the first date isn't the right time. It's good to know what you want, but you have to let yourself have a little fun too. Don't be so "modern" that you come off as intimidating. In this regard, women have lost their chivalry. We're so concerned with the "mission" that we forget to be ourselves. Men appreciate confidence, but don't overpower them with it.

2. "My priority is to create a deep connection with someone when I'm in a relationship. Marriage is something that should happen when we both feel it is right. Sure, I'd like to get married, but the person is more important to me than these ideals. I won't settle for just a person who wants to get married."

CP: If she truly wants to get married, then what she wants should be more important than what he wants. Don't settle for a person who doesn't want what you want. Stick to your ideals.

3. "I come from a divorced family, so it scares me to think that could happen to me. I want to get married, but it's more important to make sure that we are both ready to commit to a lifelong relationship and understand that there will be challenges."

CP: That's the key to marriage. It is not perfect, and there will be challenges. But if you are on the same page in terms of your commitment to work them out, you will have a great marriage. You can't go into a marriage with fear, because it will never work out.

CHAPTER 6

Law #6: *Avoid the Seven Deadly Sins of Marriage*

Shortly after getting married, I learned an important lesson: My husband and I would inevitably make mistakes, but very few mistakes—or "sins," as I call them—are worth ending the marriage for. One of the first things I learned as a newlywed, as Christopher and I ended up engaging in our first battle, was that sometimes it is better to say you're sorry and move on. This does not mean that you are backing down from your point of view or not standing up for yourself. It means that you are making things right on behalf of your marriage. Another thing I have learned from being married to my feisty Puerto Rican husband is that when I speak softly and with determination, it makes things right. It instantly deflates him. He realizes what is going on. It is as if all his feathers are up and he's ready for a fight, and then, in an instant, the moment has passed and he goes silent. That's saying a lot for a man who always has to have the last word—all the time!

Marital fights are a lot like wildfires: No matter who started the fire, someone had better suck it up and put it out or else it will escalate into something much more. Think how logical it would be to stand there, stubbornly looking for someone else to blame, while watching a small fire turning into a big one just because you weren't the one who set it. Put some water on it and move on.

I learned from my parents' example that to make a marriage last, you have to place it above your individual egos as husband and wife. If you put that commitment first, it will guide you through repairing any marriage sins that either of you may commit.

Seven Deadly Sins of Marriage

Hopefully by now you have prepared for the bond of marriage by asking yourself and your partner how you see your unique identity as a married couple. What I am about to tell you next, however, you may not be prepared for. I believe that the institution of marriage is based on S and M. Before you think I have completely lost it and have gone kinky, let me explain.

I personally believe that in the S-and-M—sadism and masochism—institution of marriage, husbands are the sadists and we wives are the masochists. Think about it for a minute. Why else would we even need marriage laws in the first place if the partnership were not composed of two such entirely different personalities coming together in a lifelong union? We need this type of guidance because, as women and men, we naturally have different ways of viewing and handling life. Men and women can be as different as night and day, and because of that marriage often requires as much maintenance as a Boeing 747.

As masochists, we women are apt to look inward and blame ourselves for the woes of the world around us. More specifically, we look for ways to place blame on ourselves for problems in our relationships, work, personal life, and anywhere else the common denominator seems to be the woman in the mirror. As sadists, men seem to have a natural instinct to blame everyone else for whatever is happening. This is not necessarily a bad thing, and I am certainly not judging them. Men simply have a more rational, logical way of viewing the world sometimes, so when something happens in their life, they look for a reasonable explanation for what has gone wrong in the relationship. Then they look around for someone else to blame.

The downside of this S-and-M way of solving relationship problems in marriages is that while the woman is looking in the mirror for a reason that the problem occurred and the man is looking everywhere else to place blame, the problem is not being solved. It is quite often festering into a bigger problem that, if left unchecked, may eventually threaten or even end the marriage. The whole point of these basic "laws" is to keep that from happening to you.

Sure, we may not have the power to change our S-and-M identities as men and women, but we do have the power to be aware of each other's tendencies, and have a set of strategies in place to avoid the most common mistakes couples make in a marriage.

I have named these mistakes the Seven Deadly Sins of Marriage. I know—first with the S-and-M kinkiness and now I am making religious references. It must be Father Alden's influence shining through. I am not saying that the traditional seven deadly sins—lust, gluttony, greed, sloth, wrath, envy, and pride—all apply to marriage. Although if you think about it, there are some connections. Depending on the situation, unchecked lust could be equated with adultery. Pride could translate into putting our own needs so far ahead of our partner's that it becomes a selfishness threatening to the marriage.

My version of the seven deadly sins, however, is focused more on what couples often do over a long period of time, often without realizing it, that eventually weakens and threatens their marriage. These marriage sins cover common marriage challenges such as how to maintain a marriage, how to handle crises, the danger in being unappreciative of your partner, and all of the other most vital day-to-day aspects of marriage that, if handled properly, will strengthen the foundation of your union.

Marriage Sin #1: Falling into Monotony

One of the biggest sins when it comes to failing to maintain a marriage is monotony. Out of monotony you lose interest in your partner; when you lose interest you lose respect; when you lose respect you lose love; and when you lose love you lose the marriage.

Do you think I'm exaggerating? It is easier than you could ever imagine for a marriage to disappear simply because we get bored. The idea of a lifetime of boredom makes a convenient excuse for those not wanting to even consider marriage, but it simply does not have to be true. Your marriage is what you make it, and it is your and your partner's job to keep things unpredictable, fun, and current.

A great example of what happens when a couple forgets to keep things unpredictable can be found in the lyrics of the popular song by Rupert Holmes called "Escape." It is one of my favorite old-school songs, and is better known as "The Piña Colada Song." I'm sure many of you have heard it and sung along with it at some point in your life. The song is about a couple who get bored with their same old relationship routine. The woman places a personal ad in the newspaper ("If you like piña coladas and getting caught in the rain . . ."). The man sees the ad and places his own ad in response ("Yes, I like piña coladas and getting caught in the rain . . ."). The two "strangers" from the personal ads set up a rendezvous ("At a bar called O'Malley's, where we'll plan our escape . . ."), and lo and behold, they each discover that the spontaneous piña-colada-and-precipitation-loving stranger is no other than their familiar (and extremely amused) partner.

How far a couple needs to go to reinvigorate their relationship and avoid monotony is up to both partners. Monotony is something that can occur very innocently at first, rearing its head in normal daily life. It can occur when a couple simply forgets to take the time to look each other in the eyes or have real conversations that bond them to each other as best friends (discussing the grocery list does not count).

Perhaps the couple is just worn down by daily life. They both get up in the morning, run out the door with their coffee, work nine to five, chauffeur the kids around, have dinner, watch television, and, too tired to do anything else, they go to bed. Their daily routine has tuned them out of life. They are both in a trance and do not realize it. Breaking out of this programming is not optional. A couple *must* make the effort to wake up and realize that their monotonous daily routine is affecting every aspect of their marriage—trust, love, sex, friendship, commitment—everything.

We are all busy. That is a given. Whether you are a stay-at-home mom, balancing a career, going to meetings, attending your kid's school events, it is hard to find the hours in the day to fit it all in. But if we fail to find the time to acknowledge our spouse and fit our marriage into our day, we are in danger of becoming nothing more than roommates, just splitting the bills. Actually there are some roommates who have more fun than some married couples who have fallen into monotony. How sad. The reason the piña colada couple looked elsewhere for excitement was that they had become boring to each other. They were no longer excited by the bond that, presumably at some point, they had worked so hard to develop.

My husband and I make it a priority to never forget this. As busy as we are as husband, wife, dad, mom, lawyer, business owner, television personality, community volunteer, and all of the other hats we each wear, we find the time to honor and enjoy each moment we can squeeze out of our busy schedules. For example, on those frequent evenings when bedtime comes and one or both of us are still

up to our eyeballs in work, our solution is to bring our laptops to bed.
I know, real romantic. But at least we are looking at each other and
talking to each other while we work. We refuse to let our daily routines
or being exhausted keep us away from spending time with each other.
And we laugh too. Have you noticed how laughing makes you just
want to kiss your mate? We realize that keeping the monotony out of
marriage is a much easier task than the alternative—letting the distance
between us grow until our marriage is in danger. It is easier to tackle
monotony.

One of the most dangerous aspects of monotony that when left
unchecked can threaten a marriage is sex. "The Piña Colada Song"
highlights one of the ways a marriage can fall into this trap.

Maintaining the sexual aspect of a marriage takes more work than
most couples may initially realize. Once the initial passion fires burn
out and life starts getting in the way, it is all too easy to forget what
attracted you to your partner in the first place. For instance, telling the
story of how I first met my husband was a great reminder of how cute
I thought he was (and still is), especially his behind. If you ever get to
the point in your marriage where you feel like sex is a chore or you just
do not see the point of making it a priority, here are some things to
remember. One—your partner might not necessarily feel the same way.
Two—remember all the butterflies in your stomach you felt when you
were first around him. It may take a minute, but once you channel
these feelings you may be surprised at how easy it is to re-create those
feelings and act on them now. Three—it is fun and pleasurable. And
four, realize the importance of making sex one of the core parts of your
marriage. Sex is a physical connection and a total connection of two
human beings like no other. It is the most intimate way that you and
your partner can strengthen your connection.

The connections between sex, romance, and love are woven tightly
into all the other aspects of marriage. One cannot exist without the
others. Sex is so much more than a physical act. I can honestly say that

after almost thirteen years of marriage, my husband is still the only person I want to have sex with.

Sex is an act of love and intimacy that strengthens the bond of marriage. Couples who deny this, and live in chronically sexless marriages, are unfortunately headed for things far worse than monotony in their marriage. Because in real life, when a bored couple decides to place and respond to personal ads, they rarely end up rendezvousing with each other.

Marriage Sin #2: Being Unappreciative

I remember a litigant on *Cristina's Court* whom I affectionately nicknamed the Lawn Mower Man. No, this was not a clever science-fiction movie reference. I called him this because his wife created so much drama and harassment in his life on a daily basis that in order to avoid it he would go out and mow the lawn (or pretend to mow the lawn). Not a bad tactic for us wives to take note of!

This couple ended up on the show as plaintiffs, suing the defendants over a contract dispute. The contract dispute, however, was definitely upstaged by the wife half of the plaintiff couple. This woman was so over-the-top high-drama and intense that it made the episode almost comical to watch. She had loaned the defendant money and for some reason assumed that the contract would be breached before it actually was.

The defendant barely had time to even think about repaying the plaintiff before Mrs. Lawn Mower Man started badgering her relentlessly for payment. Throughout the entire case, it was clear to me how embarrassed this Lawn Mower Man was to be a part of this. His life secret was now made public: He was embarrassed for letting his wife treat him like this and do this to him. It is a shame when women go to extremes like this. They have such a good thing in life and they do not appreciate it.

This story and similar others are why the next marriage sin is being unappreciative of your partner. Being unappreciative means forgetting how hard you worked to get here, to this point in your marriage, and then walking all over or taking the other person for granted; that same person you promised on your wedding day to love and honor every day of your life together.

"Till death do us part" is not some all-powerful contract that is automatically enforced just because you are married. It is up to you and your partner to maintain this promise to each other. Marriage does not forgive all sins. Couples who forget this and assume that their partner will remain by their side no matter what the circumstances and how much they are unappreciated are in danger of letting a fixable marriage sin become one that is mortal to the marriage.

Forgetting to appreciate your partner devalues your marriage and disrespects the entire history of love, trust, loyalty, respect, and life experiences that you have created with him. Ask yourself why you would risk all of these things just by forgetting to express how much you love and appreciate your spouse.

I have an enormous amount of love and appreciation for everything my husband does for me. Yes, I realize that at some points I paint a picture of my husband as a macho, obnoxious pain in the ass. Obviously, this kind of description is part tongue-in-cheek, part frustration (depending on what he did today), and, okay, partially accurate. But I am no saint either. Besides, if I really thought that he was just a pain in the ass I would not be married to him. But for all his negatives, Christopher is the most caring, loyal, affectionate, and romantic husband. He is a big contradiction. Okay, so he has brought me flowers only three times during our life together, but fortunately that is not how I judge romance.

I choose to appreciate him for his actions. His actions are undisputed evidence of how much he loves me, how proud he is of me for everything I do, and how willing he is to do whatever is needed to support our little family. I put so many demands on him, and I know I can count on him. Christopher manages all the professional responsibilities, friendships, and passions in his own life while also playing the roles of Mr. Mom while I am traveling, my publicist, personal assistant, writer, and anything else I need him for in my life.

He considers each of these roles a privilege, especially his role as Mr. Mom. He promised himself that, just like his dad, he would always be there for his kids—so he makes the time. And most important, he does not feel like his role as Mr. Mom is an attack on his manhood.

He never says no in these roles, handling these tasks that I need him for the most. He may say no about the little things in life, like getting me a glass of water or taking out the trash. But when it comes to the important things, he is always there for me without a single complaint. He may be the ultimate example of when to say no and when not to say no that I was looking for a few chapters back. He knows the difference, and I appreciate it.

But most important, my husband is my partner in life. Yes, Christopher represents the typical macho man, but that has never once gotten in the way of his pushing and encouraging me every day to be better than what I am. He is never afraid that any success I have may overshadow him. Is that self-esteem or self-confidence? I call it true love.

Our marriage is a partnership that contains two individuals willing to help each other whenever help is needed or asked for. If I did not realize all of this, I would be sinning by not appreciating him.

Marriage Sin #3: Being Dishonest

You may recall the moral of the story of how I met my husband: Being straightforward is the best way to start any relationship, especially if you want it to last. My marriage started with honesty, and I can say that my husband and I have an unblemished record of telling each other exactly what's on our minds, without holding back. I think all our friends and family know exactly what I am referring to: our honest, heated, back-and-forth cross-examination public conversations. In fact, one of our friends once said about the honest conversations Christopher and I have: "You guys always keep things real." Yes, we sure do.

We have been known to "keep things real" in public (as I mentioned in the restaurant story earlier in the book), which is perhaps not always the wisest choice, but is certainly entertaining and educational, especially for the single people out there who want a taste of marriage. For those single people who are paying attention and see my husband and me being extremely honest and straightforward with each other, I am more than happy to teach this important lesson: Marriage is not about being politically correct.

Yes, by all means, treat your spouse with respect and dignity. However, remember that this is the one person in the world whom you should be totally honest with. This should be your best friend in a sense so strong that it almost redefines the phrase *best friend* differently from anything you have ever experienced in your life. Is there anyone else in your life whom you feel as close to as your spouse and trust as much?

On *Cristina's Court*, we were visited by a newly separated couple whose marriage was irreparably divided by distrust, or more specifically, the husband's distrust of his wife. The actual case was him suing her for a computer that she allegedly promised to give him. Without a contract, this easily could have been a case of his word against hers. But the husband decided to take it upon himself to close this legal loophole. In front of the courtroom, he announced, "I have a tape recorder where she said she was going to give the computer to me. You promised me the computer and I have it here."

Well, the cheap tape-recorder gimmick worked in the short term. The wife admitted she had promised him the computer. But in the long term? This was a marriage with a serious lack of trust. She expressed how this was typical of him, and that he had been doing things like this throughout their marriage. This stated loudly and clearly how much he constantly doubted and second-guessed her. If he really did love her, then he shot himself in the foot that day for any chance of reconciliation. Because of his insecurity with himself, he didn't give love a chance.

You cannot make a marriage work in the midst of distrust and doubt in your partner. You have to be grounded in marriage and like yourself enough to join into a new life with somebody else.

When you distrust or are dishonest with your spouse, you are adding an element of distance to your relationship. Each time that you keep a secret, tell a half truth, or engage in some other lie to your partner, you are unknowingly adding a brick to the wall that will inevitably grow between the two of you. Incidentally, I am not talking about little white lies and incidentals, like the shoes or purse you just bought without telling your husband. Husbands don't need to know how many pairs of shoes or purses we really have. I'm talking about the really big things in life: the things where your gut instinct as a woman tells you that if he knew what you were keeping from him, he would be hurt by your actions.

"Keeping it real" may not always be pretty, and in many situations that you will encounter in your marriage, it will require some inner strength. But ultimately, when you choose honesty over dishonesty in your marriage, it is a testament to your strength as a woman and a sign of how strong your marriage is.

Marriage Sin #4: Going Nuclear

Have you ever been in the middle of a heated argument with your spouse and instinctively sensed that the next words out of your mouth—the ones on the tip of your tongue that you *know* you want to say to him—will likely ignite a nuclear war of sorts in your marriage?

Most likely, the thing that stopped you in your tracks was the awareness that once you push the theoretical red button there is no taking it back. And once you press your red button the other person in the argument has unspoken permission to press theirs, and suddenly your marriage has been reduced to a wasteland. That is why I call this marriage sin *going nuclear.*

I have my own "going nuclear" story from my own marriage that is still embarrassing to own up to, even all these years later, because of how much I love my husband and what a fool I made of myself. One time early in our marriage, Christopher and I had an explosive argument that started with an issue so petty I honestly do not remember what it was. This is proof of how hard it is to see the big fights coming any more than the little ones. Any fight can become "the big one" if both partners are not aware of what they are saying and how they are escalating the fight. For me, this was one of those fights.

Maybe it's because it was very early on in our marriage. I was still learning the rules of the game, ground rules for arguments and pacing out the new boundaries of our relationship. We both still had a lot to learn about where the line is drawn between speaking up and saying things you can't take back.

This fight was just horrible, and it got out of control so quickly. Suddenly I found myself threatening my husband, the man I love and respect, with divorce. I actually used these words: "Why don't you just leave?" To which he responded, "If you want me to, I will!" We had reached the point of no return, and I suddenly saw in his eyes how much I had wounded him. Seeing that kind of hurt on my husband's face has stuck with me since that day, now almost thirteen years later. I don't think I could do or say anything like that ever again in our lifetime. In fact, I do not think I could even use the word *divorce* with my husband, especially as a weapon in a fight, ever again. In a flash moment of anger and in my irrational mind I may have thought that using that word would help me win the argument. Why was I trying to make my husband lose an argument in the first place? This whole situation resulted in nothing more than awful feelings about myself and questions of how I could be so immature and stupid. It taught me a lesson much more than it affected him, and he got over it faster than I did.

In the next few pages, I will tell you various other stories of much less serious battles and bickering from my marriage, many of them comical. The reason I opened with this story is to impress upon you the importance of being aware of what you are saying and whom you are saying it to—your partner in love and marriage.

Women are allowed to get upset with their husbands once in a while (or more often), and vice versa. Every marriage has its own boundaries, with rules agreed upon by each partner. The longer you are married, the more accustomed you are to navigating these rules; you learn to fight fair, and in some cases you even establish a rhythm. For instance, I have noticed in my own marriage how arguments that used to take an hour now take about thirty seconds. My husband and I apply all our cross-examination skills that come from being lawyers and get from problem to resolution in record time these days. I think we have both learned how to weed through the nonsense. We've had to, because there are so many other things in life to enjoy.

This familiarity is also the result of the love and trust that build as the marriage grows. We have earned the safety net that allows us to go out of bounds once in a while without earning a penalty. The other thing I have learned is that the longer I am married, the more I learn to be selective about which things I am willing to go to battle over. If I were not selective, I would probably be insane by now! The point is, as long as we keep everything honest and straightforward, a few emotional outbursts once in a while are not marriage killers.

However, what if your partner just pushes you too far into the "going nuclear" zone and there are barely any words to describe your anger? I don't know about you, but I will be the first to admit that my husband knows how to push my buttons. I have been in disbelief several times during our marriage. There have been moments when I have thrown up my hands and said, "Did you really just say that to me?" On many occasions I have wondered what on earth my husband must be thinking.

Here is a personal example of a situation that might have driven someone else over the edge, but one in which I managed to find the humor. I am sure countless women have experienced situations just like it with their own husbands. Picture this: It has been an extremely long workday, full of appointments, interviews, never-ending phone calls (usually on multiple phones at once), errands, and various other back-to-back responsibilities. I have just dashed in the door and soon I am on another business call while, at the same time, I tidy up the house and start figuring out dinner while spending time with our daughter. The call waiting clicks in. It is Christopher. I put my call on hold, thinking that my husband is calling to quickly let me know he is on his way home. He's on his way home, all right—and with several of his out-of-town buddies, having promised them dinner and an entertaining evening with his charming hostess wife (me). I am standing there with the phone in my hand, wearing the sweats I threw on after dashing in the door, and with no idea of what kind of dinner I am supposed to whip up. I am in absolute disbelief. This may be a not-so-extreme example, but it definitely shows how the seeds of going nuclear can be sown by letting everyday stresses build up.

This is an example of times when I get so upset at my husband that all I can do is laugh, as a way of maintaining my sanity, if nothing else (and have a glass of wine in the middle of it all). Laughing is a much better choice than going over the edge and getting as mad as you know you could be in the situation. When faced with these problems or situations, you just need to ask yourself, "Is this something I am going to get divorced over or can I just get over it and move on?" Is it so serious and disrespectful to you and your marriage that it is worth losing your spouse over? Think about it. Not many of our everyday marital problems are, so we need to deal with them in perspective.

There are times in every marriage when the you-know-what hits the fan and emotions on both sides are running at peak intensity. These are the most important times to put on the brakes, take a deep breath, and weigh your priorities. Ask yourself how important proving your point or having the last word is. Be honest with yourself about how much you are willing to risk for the sake of being right. Do this before either you or your partner says or does something you cannot take back. Choose your words carefully and pick what you really want to say. Select the words that matter the most to you, because if you do not you may say something that even the deepest regret cannot take back.

When you are pushed to the edge for one reason or another, ask yourself what your marriage is worth to you. This is a lesson my mother taught me. I view my parents' marriage as an example of the ultimate commitment and of how to tough it out through far worse daily crises than this. My mother taught me that marriage is about hanging in there, especially through the tough times, because that is what you promised. So, as I stand there in my sweats, looking around the kitchen for ideas—and in utter disbelief—I then heed my mother's advice. Instead of going nuclear, I laugh, because in the course of any marriage there could very well be tougher times than unexpected dinner guests. And by the way, I ordered in that night. But I will take credit for the lovely cheese-and-fruit platter.

When you love someone as much as you (hopefully) love your spouse, you are going to feel strong, often overwhelming emotions toward them. This is a part of life and definitely a part of marriage. Even if you do occasionally go over the edge and go nuclear on your spouse, the important thing is to find a way to get some perspective as soon as possible. This perspective could come from laughter, sleeping apart for a night, or just taking a deep, cleansing breath. However you do it, just make sure you and your partner establish some sort of release valve on the pressure cooker so the lid doesn't blow.

Marriage Sin #5: Being His Mother

Okay, this is *my* biggest marriage sin. I admit it. But I get better every day. I ask my husband to do something and I literally give him one second to do it. It's as if I assume it will not get done if it does not get done *now*. I want things done now, and I want them done my way, because I am a perfectionist. There is that S&M rearing its ugly head again.

Let me put it this way: My husband used to have a *lot* more chores than he has now. My perfectionism has created a monster, and now I do most everything around the house. Two of Christopher's major remaining chores are putting out the empty water bottles for replacement ones, and taking the garbage out. Even after all our years of marriage, I have still found myself reminding him (multiple times) every Thursday night to take the garbage out. "Please take out the garbage, Christopher." "I'll do it after dinner." A half hour later: "Don't forget the garbage, Chris." "In a minute." After years of nagging, I discovered that I was driving *myself* crazy. I don't know that my nagging was having much of an effect on my husband, but I was losing my mind keeping up my nagging responsibilities.

If I took a poll of all husbands and all of my male friends, I guarantee they would list nagging as women's worst downfall, without a close second. So finally I decided to stop nagging. I asked myself what the worst thing was that could happen. I made peace with the image in my mind of the garbage and empty water bottles piling up, week after week. I imagined being completely surrounded by garbage and realized that my marriage was still more important.

So now I do not say a word. I don't care. I realized that it will not make or break my life if the garbage waits another week (God willing it is only one week). My rule of thumb is that the third reminder is officially nagging. The first time he probably did not hear you. The second time he definitely heard you. Before you remind him the third time, stop, breathe, and channel Dirty Harry. Ask yourself, Do you feel lucky? The "one, two, three" rule is the rule I live by, and I am happy with it because it works.

My own perfectionist tendencies and Dirty Harry aside, women in general have the tendency to want everything *now!*—whether it is a response to our comment that shows our spouse was listening to us, an answer to our question, or when we want something done. Women seem to have a natural need for instant gratification, and all too often, our partners are on the receiving end of this urgency.

Perhaps this is because, as young girls, we learned this from our mothers and grandmothers. Think about how many times we saw how effective nagging could be in lighting a fire under a man's behind. I personally think that there were a whole lot of overworked, overwhelmed women who found it easier to treat their husbands and children the same way—just for the sake of efficiency and to keep the household running efficiently, with everyone pulling their weight.

This kind of impatience and nagging becomes a marriage sin when we take it to extremes. If you take an impatient attitude and a tendency to constantly nag too far, you can turn from your spouse's wife into his mother in mere moments. Since your husband already has a mother, you can see how this could become a problem in your marriage. Taking on the mothering role is the farthest thing possible from the smart, sexy woman your husband thought he was marrying.

Remember this the next time the third reminder to your husband to take out the garbage is just on the tip of your tongue. Trust that he heard you the first two times. I have developed a theory along these lines: that men live in a different time zone than we do as women. I developed this theory long ago, but it is reinforced every day. For example, one evening I asked my husband if he would bring me a glass of wine. I was working tirelessly on a project and I had just delved into a new idea. I asked Christopher politely, and he said that yes, he would be happy to bring me a glass of wine. Exactly forty-eight minutes later (yes, I counted), I got my wine. I had two choices—I could either bite my lip and say thank you or bite his head off and ask him whether he actually went out and traveled to a local winery to get my glass of wine. I asked myself, *What good will it possibly do to get angry? What will this accomplish?* So I smiled, said thank you, and accepted the glass. Although truthfully I was worried that if I nagged him about it, next time forty-eight minutes might become a few hours!

Marriage Sin #6: Forsaking Him

The sixth deadly sin of marriage is forsaking your spouse, and therefore your marriage. A friend of my mom's once told me, "You have to make your husband the top priority in your life." This may sound like you are treating your family unequally but it is true. Your children are paramount and obviously need love and attention. But if you do not respect the delicate balance of marriage and family, and make your husband the priority, you and your husband are in danger of becoming strangers once the kids grow up and leave. I hear about couples who have been married for twenty or thirty years and suddenly get divorced, and I wonder if this sixth deadly sin of marriage contributed to the demise of such a long, seemingly solid union.

At some point during the marriage, usually when the kids are little and require the most attention, it is easy to trade in your identities as wife and husband for new identities as mom and dad. Instead of learning to balance the new roles, you simply trade away the old ones— husband, wife, lover, partner, best friend, and confidant. You take it for granted that you can assume those identities again at a moment's notice. But in the meantime, it is not okay to leave your marriage self rusting in the corner of the shed like an old lawn mower.

If you have forsaken your marriage for your kids or for your life in general, that means you have not been working to maintain it. Marriage takes work. Everything you promised each other on your wedding day cannot and *should not* go out the window just because you have taken on new roles in life—whether those roles are mom and dad, new career hats, or anything else that gets in the way of your marriage.

You may still believe in your heart that once the kids leave the nest, you and your spouse will instantly become newlyweds again, with all the passion, love, lust, trust, and an equally strong bond holding your marriage together. Unfortunately, it does not always work that way. Once you abandon your marriage it is hard to reestablish that bond. If you stop talking to your best friend of twenty years there will be no marriage left, much less any sexual attraction. Even when you and your partner finally do decide to step back into your identities as husband and wife, the marriage you come back to may not be the same one you remember.

Marriage Sin #7: Losing Your Identity

Before my husband and I were married, we each had our own separate lives and our own identities within those lives. Golf, for instance, has always been a big—okay, *huge*—part of Christopher's life. I knew this when I married him. He plays on sunny days, cloudy days, weekdays, weekends, on back-to-back days, and every other chance he gets in between. In addition to golf, my husband spends a great deal of time on the phone and going out with his friends. I have learned to be patient, understanding, and give him his space. The more space you give your spouse, the more you will want to be with and appreciate each other.

Remember my story about how Christopher and I split for a time before finally deciding to get married? Well, I later found out that he continued playing golf with my father the whole time during our breakup! This is why I always joke that golf is like my husband's first wife and I am his mistress. Honestly, I have no complaints. Like I said, I already knew this about him before we got married; I accepted it, and I realize that golf is a significant part of my husband's individual identity, as is his strong bond with his friends. He's a guy's guy. I do not see this as a threat to our marriage at all. When he is golfing, he is doing his thing, and I am off doing mine. I actually love and thoroughly enjoy this time when we each pursue our own interests. You cannot be around someone twenty-four hours a day, no matter how much you love and adore your partner. You need a breather to collect your own thoughts and do the things that you have always enjoyed doing (hobbies, interests, clubs, groups, etc.). Just like you need time alone from your best friend sometimes, you need a break from your best friend in life. When my husband and I are apart, we are separate yet together. We have become a "we" who respect each other's time. We have found a way to balance the "I" and "we" of marriage.

I say this because there is a misconception that with marriage comes the loss of your individual identity as a woman as you become a "we" and leave your "I" at the altar. I have found the complete opposite to be true. Whereas there is compromise in the day-to-day realities of marriage, there should never be compromise of the unique identities that have come together. You can compromise on some things but never your identity. Marriage should never be a drain on or a threat to your identity—it should strengthen it.

There was once a beautiful, gorgeous, vibrant woman. She was the life of the party and had a busy dating and social life. She had a strong sense of self. That is, until one particular guy came along and had a disturbingly powerful effect on her identity. I say this because this woman is my friend, and watching her transformation from fabulous to frumpy as soon as she started dating this particular person was upsetting. Suddenly, my friend "Hot Latina Barbie" was dressing in formless shirts and long skirts, covering all those beautiful curves and femininity. Even more significantly, she was not the loud, vivacious, fun woman I knew and loved. It was almost like she went into a coma. The shell was there but not her, as far as identity is concerned. Understand, it wasn't her physical appearance that gave her this magnetism, made her dynamic, and made people gravitate toward her. It was her personality and her identity. The physical was an extension of the strength of identity that was radiating from the inside outward.

She let this man completely change that. He had a strange kind of control over her where he completely robbed her blind of her identity, and she changed as a result of it. She went so far, so blindly into this relationship that she became engaged to him. But she was not truly in love and one day she snapped out of it. She realized how far she had traveled away from her identity, asked herself what on earth she was doing, and, shortly after the breakup, she became herself again.

Marriage is an incredible union of two unique people coming together and creating a life together, but without losing the uniqueness of the two people in the process. I do not see any individuality getting lost in the bond of marriage. It cannot. I see it amplified, magnified, and exaggerated in a way that makes you more acutely aware of who you are as an individual than ever before in your life. Marriage makes each partner the absolute best version of themselves. And a good partner celebrates and encourages the other's identity instead of making them hide or change a unique piece of themselves.

Being married also forces you to truly define and refine yourself as an individual, as a woman, and as a human being. As a person you become stronger in who you are and what you want. You realize what is really valuable to you and what is not. Marriage helps you confront exactly what your priorities are in life. Those priorities extend to a whole new set of roles that you take on in marriage—wife, mother, and representative of a new family unit. With each new hat, you gain more pieces of your identity.

My husband and I may not be perfect as individuals, but we are somehow perfect together. We have always developed our own separate identities in a way that is independent of each other while also being dependent on each other as a married couple. I have not lost who I am and neither has my husband. Because our individual identities strengthen our marriage identity our marriage is a complete and perfect union.

For Keeps

Hopefully these seven sins and marriage laws have shown you how a union as good as marriage requires maintenance. This is a never-ending task. Marriage is something you have to take care of. Do not fall into the common trap that has you and your partner thinking, *Now that we are Mr. and Mrs., all the hard work is over.* The fact is that on your wedding day, the hard work is just beginning. But it is the good kind of hard work—the kind that leads to the best things in life.

Maintaining a bond as strong as marriage is like taking care of a plant—if you forget to water it one day it will be dead the next. And in the case of marriage, that death means divorce. This is obviously a touchy subject for some couples for a variety of reasons, such as past divorces of parents, family members, or friends; or one spouse's past divorces; religious beliefs on the subject; fear of loss or being alone; or all the other reasons that make divorce one of the most stressful things that can happen to us as human beings.

"Till death do you part" may seem like a rather old-fashioned expression in our world today, but for me, it remains the only way to approach a marriage. The reason that I personally find it almost impossible to enter the word *divorce* into my vocabulary has to do with the values my parents taught me about marriage. Couples in older generations, like my parents, knew the importance of choosing love, staying with the relationship, and never giving up.

And, based on my near-divorce story I shared with you earlier, it is my conviction that I married the right person, who has carried me through all the ups and downs of marriage. I have no doubts. I know he's the right person for me, and every single day of my life that feeling gets stronger.

This is important to note, because sometimes people get married for the wrong reasons. In some cases, it is a marriage of convenience, made up of two people who are settling for each other for fear that this is the best they can ask for or deserve.

I overheard an example of this one time while Chris and I were at dinner. Three couples were having the "let's all talk about how we met" discussion. One couple's story in particular made my ears perk up. I felt bad about eavesdropping, but let's face it, in some restaurants the tables are placed so close together you feel like you should introduce yourself to your neighbors.

Anyway, the wife described how she met her husband and at first was not really that into him, but eventually saw him as a quality guy (was she car shopping?). She admitted that she was not attracted to him at first, but her mom really liked him and he came from a great family. So essentially, she settled. I wondered how he felt listening to that.

This made me wonder how many people really know what they are doing when they get married, and understand it. The right reasons to get married come from a genuine, honest place. They include truly loving, respecting, and understanding *why* you want to spend the rest of your life with this person and actually seeing a future life together with him that you could not have with anyone else. You both have put serious thought into the decision, whether your life goals match, and whether you share the desire and love to make this commitment and move forward. I believe that people who settle or do not get married for any of the other right reasons are giving themselves excuses to give up on the marriage before they even walk down the aisle.

This is especially disturbing, since my parents taught me that you cannot just toss aside your marriage—and all the love, trust, and commitment built within it—just because things do not seem to be going your way. They taught me that, as a married couple, you work on your problems together, because your marriage is far more important than any problem you will ever face in life. My mother has always reminded me that marriage is a sacred vow, with love, mutual respect, understanding, and patience as the keys to maintaining it for life.

Marriage should never be taken casually. Young people especially need to be taught the difference between the instant gratification of the latest gadget, Web site, or piece of technology and the institution of marriage. In marriage the only "upgrades" are anniversary milestones, and "social networking" is what occurs in the bedroom during lovemaking, in the kitchen during meal making, and in the family room as you make time for the most important "action item" in your life—maintaining your marriage.

The decision to get divorced is a serious one and should never be taken lightly, as if it is just a fork in the road and you're choosing to go down one side or the other. Obviously there are some serious problems that cannot be overcome, and only you can be the judge of that. But with divorce you are making the decision to break the vow that you made to your partner on your wedding day. You are choosing to give up on the love and commitment that you once had toward each other, and admitting that the problems in your relationship have defeated that love, once and for all.

If this is truly a decision you are about to make, please do yourself, your partner, and your marriage a favor and think outside the box. Look outside the things that are dividing the two of you right now and see the bigger picture. Do you really think that couples who have been married for over fifty years have never gone through what you are going through now—or even worse? Just because you are not feeling love for your partner now does not mean that your love has died. Something drew the two of you together, and now you are being tested to see if you can both remember what that is and how to rekindle it.

Ultimately, if you are contemplating divorce, the only way that you are going to make it through this time is by finding a larger purpose to why you and your spouse came together in the first place. Your marriage is a much stronger connection than you may realize. Think about the consequences to your identity before you sever that connection. Also remember that divorce is never to be considered as a solution for your own personal insecurities or internal problems you may have connecting with your identity.

My identity is firmly connected to my marriage. I do not give up on my marriage because my husband is my best friend. He is a part of my identity that I cannot sacrifice. I have learned through experience that it sometimes takes an incredible amount of work to maintain a good marriage. But, as my parents taught me, marriage is about forging a connection with my husband that cannot be broken because it is rooted in who I am. He is a part of me, and therefore if our marriage died, a huge piece of my identity would die with it. Not only do I love and adore my husband, but I also really trust him. But it goes both ways. This is hard for some people to really accept.

I can only hope that by your taking to heart the information in this chapter and, if nothing else, just working to maintain an honest, open bond with your spouse, divorce is something that you and your partner will never have to face.

Above all, remember these marriage laws, especially in times of crisis, to keep this wonderful union—your marriage—healthy, happy, and strong. Marriage requires straightforward communication, nurturing, acute awareness, and everything else required to make *your* marriage work. You and your spouse worked so hard and undoubtedly endured so many other relationships and breakups to get to this point. Never forget what you went through to find this person and create this eternal bond. Marriage is not the finish line. It is the beginning of a whole new race.

My Verdict

A good marriage is one that allows each partner to have the complete freedom to be individuals, together yet separate. In marriage, becoming a "we" is not a bad thing at all—as long as you do not lose your "I."

"IN HER OWN WORDS"

I asked some smart, confident women to share their thoughts on the laws covered in this chapter. Here is what they said, along with my responses.

How do you maintain your identity within your marriage?

1. "I still do all the things I enjoyed before I was married. I still have the same friends as I did when I was single, and I enjoy plenty of time away from my husband. That's how I maintain my identity in marriage."

CP: Exactly! This is one of the keys to a successful marriage.

2. "You need to have some alone time. Having hobbies that you enjoy on your own is important."

CP: If you don't like being by yourself or are not comfortable with yourself, how can you be good company to anyone else?

3. "Our ability to love unconditionally is one of the greatest gifts we bring into our marriage."

CP: This *is* one of the greatest gifts of marriage because of that security that comes from knowing you now have a partner who has accepted you for you and made a vow to love you under the best and worst circumstances as long as you both shall live.

4. "I have learned that my husband is not my best girlfriend, so I should never try to make him into that—he has no interest in playing that role. He is my best friend, but in a completely different way."

CP: Yes, of course. It is about recognizing your role. Your husband is a different kind of best friend, because it's a different relationship. This is an important point for people to differentiate.

CHAPTER 7

Law #7: *Be Smart and Successful in Friendship*

I learned the true value of genuine, lasting friendship from the Dukes. Back in the days when countless lifelong friendships were formed and nurtured on the streets and stoops of inner cities, a group of guys came together and called themselves the Dukes. The guys emerged on the scene of inner-city life in the 1950s, some native born and others immigrants. The city was New York and one of those Dukes was my beloved father-in-law, Ray Gonzalez, son of Puerto Rican immigrant parents. He was the Duke named Pee Wee, because he was the shortest. There was also Whitey (the only white Duke), Flunky (flunked out of school), Shadow (the sole black Duke), and the Irish, Dominican, and Puerto Rican Dukes.

This was a remarkable mixture of friends, especially during a time in New York and urban America in general when city blocks were segregated by ethnicity. In a neighborhood where crossing the street could easily result in a territorial spat, the Dukes managed to transcend the petty differences that separate people, and came together instead. Although just like any other gang, and not unlike the ones in *West Side Story*, they fought their battles. But that was how things were, and friendships lasted far longer than grudges.

Even though he was the smallest Duke, Ray was the group leader. He took that role seriously, holding the group together for over fifty years, through military service, jobs, cross-country moves, wives, kids, grandkids, and all the other life events that often separate old friends. But Ray kept his Dukes close to him throughout his life, treating their unique friendship with respect and love, and forging a genuine bond among friends unlike any I have ever seen.

He named Whitey (real name Sidney) as my husband's godfather. Ray and Sidney's friendship was truly remarkable. You would have thought they were blood brothers. Ray, Sidney, and all the Dukes were their own little family, and their family extended into ours. At our wedding, they made my father, Dario, an honorary Duke, and they still call my husband, Christopher, "Duke."

None of the Dukes ever forgot Ray's role in helping keep the group together over all those years. So when Ray fell ill with cancer, the Dukes were there to pick him up. From the moment they arrived at his bedside calling out, "Hey, Pee Wee," to when they carried his coffin at the funeral, the bond between these lifelong friends was inspiring. When Ray died, it was as if a big part of the heart of the Dukes' friendship stopped beating.

The Casualness of Friendship

I realize how unfair it would be to compare most friendships to the Dukes'. Very few people are able to keep their friends that close and, even through the turmoil of life, never let them go. What percentage of friendships today can we honestly say even come close to this level of commitment? I hear some of us hemming and hawing sometimes, when trying to determine whether someone is a best friend, a friend, or an acquaintance. Have you noticed that we actually have a hierarchy of friendship, divided into these categories? If we cannot say with certainty that someone is our friend, then is that a friendship of convenience or of substance? A friendship of convenience is when people become friends because one or both of them need something—validation, social stature, or anything else that makes a friendship casual and expendable when those needs are met. It is when your "friends" are yes people who say only what they think you want to hear and what will keep them in your favor. There is no deep bond when such superficialities hold together a friendship. When you add the element of casualness to friendships, you subtract the heart of the friendship.

This is because our friendships are such a key piece of our identities as women. There is a part of us as women that naturally seeks to forge deep connections with other people—our girlfriends, spouses, family, and children. When we deny that and allow our friendships to be casual and convenient, we deny who we are as women. This is not to say that men do not share this need. For instance, Christopher clearly learned the value of friendship from his father, Ray, the Duke. My husband keeps his friends close to him. He has had one particular friend since he moved from New York to California at the age of six. He learned that friendships mean something only if you give them meaning, and he has made the choice to do that, just as I have made that choice in my own friendships.

I have learned that friendships require the same communication, maintenance, honesty, nurturing, and attention as a marriage. Just as couples cannot miraculously stay married without putting the work in, people cannot expect a friend to continue being there for them without investing anything into the relationship. I will admit that I am a big friendship investor. If friendship were the stock market, I would have alternately gained and lost millions over the years. I have a good radar for people, but I also see the best in people. This has led to occasional moments of betrayal, but overall it has led me to invest the very best of myself in nurturing and sustaining my true friendships, and never expecting a thing in return. I would go beyond the extra mile for each of my friends, and they know it. Our friendships are an unspoken bond, and there is never a question of whether we will be there for one another.

There are countless examples of how my friends have been there for me when I have needed them the most. Here, however, is an example of how I have attempted to repay their loving generosity the best I could.

I call my best friend by the name Chula, which means "cutie" in Mexico, and she calls me the same in return. She even calls my husband Chulo and my daughter Chulita—we are the *chula* family. Chula has been my best friend for over fifteen years. We met as friends, working for two separate wonderful bosses who even commented on our similarities, stating to each other, "We both have Cristinas working in our offices!"

Our friendship is easy to maintain. I don't have to call her every day because we have an ageless sense of our friendship that is unspoken. I feel blessed to be a part of her group of friends because I know I am part of a small, exclusive group of old-school friends whom she has kept close to her for many years. We are always there for each other, and the friendship never feels like work because it is genuine. A dedication I once wrote about Chula says it all about our friendship: *Thank you to my girlfriend Chula, for her constant belief in me. She is a source of support and is the perfect embodiment of one of my favorite sayings—True friendship is one soul shared by two bodies.*

When I make friends with someone, as I did with Chula long ago, their family becomes part of my family and vice versa. I knew that Chula's father was ill, but I did not know how serious it was until she called and told me, "If you want to see him, you need to see him now." It did not matter that every minute of my day was scheduled. All that mattered was getting in my car and going to her.

A friend in need has the power to wipe away all the millions of things on your plate in an instant. With true friendship there are no tests, and you never have to prove anything. Instead, in moments like this the friendship proves itself. There are no excuses or rationalizations in friendship. There is just showing up when your friend needs you. With true friendships, there is no doubt as to whether you are friends or acquaintances, and there is nothing casual about it.

Yet there are still people out there among us who say they have the closest friendships in the world. But their actions do not match their words. There were three female litigants on *Cristina's Court* who claimed to be as close as sisters, and swore up and down how much they loved one another. One night these three "friends like sisters" went out drinking at a bar. The designated-driver friend got a little drunk, the two other friends decided to take off to a party, and the drunk designated driver was about to be left behind. The two other friends noticed a guy whom they all knew at the bar and decided that he qualified as a ride home for their designated-driver friend. The problem was that she had past issues with this guy and was uncomfortable with him, and they knew it. They also knew that she might have been too drunk to know what was going on, but they left her anyway. He told them he would drive her home. Instead, he took her out to the parking lot and raped her in her own car.

She called her "friends" the next day, beyond livid for what they had done to her. They were not the least bit remorseful that day or the day they came to court. One of their "best friends" had been raped, and all they were doing was pointing fingers and spinning accusations. I was in disbelief that throughout this, they continued to refer to one another as friends. Because friends do not point accusing fingers. Friends trust and forgive and keep each other safe. We stay safe in this world because of our true friends. These women, despite their extremely misguided beliefs, were not friends. And that is how a casual friendship can be dangerous to your well-being.

Woman Versus Woman

There is a widely held theory that women are incapable of having the kind of nonjudgmental friendships men have. We are often accused of letting jealousy, cattiness, and competition invade the bonds of our friendships. Curious to find out what women thought of this theory, I asked various women if they thought women or men were more capable of maintaining friendships. Their responses are scattered throughout this chapter. I was a little surprised at the divide in answers. Some women stated in no uncertain terms that, yes, men are better at friendships, while others vehemently disagreed. Why the split?

Remember what I said about marriage being an S&M relationship because men and women approach it in such different ways? Well, friendships are the same. A friendship between men is a lot lower-maintenance than one between women. They do not require as many phone calls and as much checking in as women do in their friendships. This absolutely does not mean that men do not have to work at maintaining their friendships. They just do it differently than women do. I mentioned that my husband learned valuable lessons of friendship from his father, and Christopher has subsequently maintained several deep and lasting friendships in his life. If maintenance were not an issue, he would not be able to do this. Men also do not seem to have the jealousy aspect to their friendships that women often have. If their buddy has something they do not, they don't see it as a personal reflection on their shortfalls. Their only competition is the man in the mirror. Men are islands in that regard, and I will admit it—sometimes I'm jealous of this.

The jealousy aspect of women's relationships comes from insecurity with our own identities. The way that this insecurity plays into our friendships works in a cycle. When we are younger, especially in high school and college, proximity to lots of friendship options creates lifelong bonds. We are young, trusting, and hungry for emotional and intellectual connections with others. As we create our identities and find our place in the world, there is an enormous number of questions to explore. I have nothing but sympathy for the folks in college dorms responsible for noise control. When young women convene, the conversations can last for days! As we explore and learn about life together, entire pieces of our identity are formed and bonds are created with the friends who help make it happen. It's easy to believe, at this point in our lives, that it will always be this easy to form these types of deep, emotional friendships. Everyone is on an equal playing field.

However, once college ends and the game of life begins, the playing field is no longer even, and it's every woman for herself. We whip out the yardstick and start noticing who gets her dream job first, who makes the most money, who gets married first, who has kids, who moves into her dream home, and other external factors that women judge themselves and one another based on. What's really happening is that in their twenties, after college, women are developing a new, independent piece of their identity. Unfortunately, many see their girlfriends as threats to this independence, rather than sources of support for it. They watch their girlfriends gain success faster and they feel threatened, especially when they do not see that success in their own life.

This is all based entirely on perception, external accomplishments, and other things that truly do not matter when it comes to friendship. It's time we put down the yardstick and started focusing on our own accomplishments without constantly comparing ourselves to our friends. Because comparison leads to competition, competition leads to jealousy, and suddenly the bond of friendship has been needlessly shattered.

Fortunately (and hopefully not too late for some friendships), by the time we reach our thirties, most of us realize this. By this point in life, hopefully we know who we are, we see what we have accomplished, and we know how to separate accomplishments from identity. We are not our job, our house, our car, the fact that we have a husband, how many kids we have, or the balance in our savings account, and neither are our friends. We learn the value of true friendship. Generally, once we get older we stop obsessing about the material things and we recognize and accept our friends for who they are and the valuable role they play in our life.

For example, my best friend, Chula, whom I mentioned earlier in this chapter, is single. Yet, even in her singleness, she is not at all threatened by the fact that my life as a married person is different from hers. I have a husband and child; she does not, and honestly, who cares? I know she would love to have a husband and child, but she doesn't let that consume or torture her to the point where she is uncomfortable being around us or unable to enjoy our company. She is not afraid to incorporate herself into my life, and respects my identity as a wife and mother, without seeing it as a threat to her own. She does not use that one aspect of my identity as an excuse that gets in the way of our friendship.

Once we all understand that one woman's accomplishments are not another woman's failures we will be able to demolish this unfortunate reputation of cattiness, "girl fights," jealousy, and all the other things that stand in the way of deep, fulfilling friendships that last a lifetime.

Men and Women As Friends

When Harry met Sally in the movie of the same name, one of the first things he told her was that there was no way a man and a woman could have a platonic relationship. I beg to differ. Humberto Rafael Gray, or

HRG, as I call him, was my first boss; he is my crazy Dominican friend, and I even joke that he is my "other husband" because he is genuinely my best guy friend. He is a gorgeous man, a brilliant lawyer, businessman, husband, and human being, a good mentor in many ways.

He is there for me no matter what is happening in my life, and I can count on him for anything. There is not one issue we cannot talk about, just as I would with my friend Chula. I can cry to him, I can be ridiculous with him, I can laugh, I can ask for advice, and he is completely nonjudgmental, and he always has my best interests in mind, with nothing in it for him. There is such a genuine and real bond between us, it is really hard to put into words what our friendship means to me. Luckily, I asked Humberto for some help and he described our friendship beautifully. Read his words carefully, because within them are all the principles of a genuine, loving, unconditional friendship.

"Delineating and defining what a 'friendship' is requires time. Only over time can you truly understand and get to know a person. After years of knowing you, our friendship is evolving every day and becoming stronger. I always joke when I meet someone new who wants to immediately be our best friend, and they try to penetrate our circle, that I will talk to them again and assess our friendship in ten years. Sometimes you have new relationships where you hit it off quickly, but you don't invest time with that person and they really never become a close friend. Years later, without realizing it, do you say to yourself, 'Wow, do you realize we have been close friends for twenty years now?' Friendship also requires respect! I think this is why we are still the best of friends. I have always tried to recognize and keep separate friendship and business. I understand the line! This is why it was never crossed. I recognize the line between friendship and friends with benefits. My respect for you is too great to cross it! I always put our friendship first. I cherish it and respect it. This is why I keep distinct boundaries. To do otherwise compromises friendship, which ultimately leads to the end of the friendship."

Humberto is absolutely right about the danger in blurring lines within a friendship. There is not and has never been any romance or sexual attraction between Humberto and me. We have never come anywhere near that invisible boundary that divides friend and lover. This is a nonissue. We are the best of friends and we do not see the fact that we are man and woman as related to the depth of our friendship. It is wonderful to have that kind of friendship without limitations.

Here is an example of how my friendship with Humberto can be just as perplexing to outsiders as it is special to us. One night, Humberto came to my house to pick me up for one of our "friendship dates" that we sometimes go on, just as I would with any of my girlfriends. We went to one of our favorite restaurants and, as usual, caught up on the details of our lives, from our respective marriages and families to our businesses and everything else in between.

We didn't think anything of it—a man and a woman, both wearing wedding bands, laughing and sharing personal stories with obvious familiarity—because we have been close friends for so long. It just seems natural and normal to us. But we realized that perhaps the rest of the world didn't see it quite this way when the waiter asked Humberto if he wanted to order for his wife. We laughed at the idea that a friendship like ours, that transcends gender, is apparently rare in nature.

The waiter's comment sparked the first conversation that Humberto and I ever had about why we never felt the urge to cross the line as a man and a woman, especially considering how close we are in every other aspect of our lives. It's not that we do not find each other physically attractive—we are both human, after all. But our physical *appreciation* for each other never once came close to turning into a *desire* for each other. We finally concluded over dinner that night that the love and respect we have for each other as friends is so paramount that the idea of a physical relationship never even emerged.

This kind of platonic relationship between a man and a woman is especially uncomplicated when we are secure with ourselves and understand the meaning of true friendship. That way there is no question of accidentally crossing the line into the romance zone. I think we get a bad rap as women when it comes to our ability to recognize the difference between friendship and something more.

This also comes with maturity. In college, sometimes the line is blurred (there are many blurry lines in college), and trying to maintain a platonic relationship with clear-cut boundaries can be risky. When you are older you learn that the idea of "friends with benefits" is ridiculous and childish. It is not a friendship and there are certainly no benefits.

I value all my friendships, regardless of whether they are with men or women. But my best friend in the world will always be my husband.

Basic Friendship Lessons

There are some important lessons about friendship that I am eager to teach my daughter Sofia as soon as the time is right. There are also some lessons that I am already teaching her now, as she finds her way through the earliest friendships that children develop. Regardless of when I teach her these lessons, I realize that some aspects of children's friendships have changed, simply because times change. However, as I mentioned in a previous chapter about dating, as quickly as things change, some things remain the same. This applies to the basic rules of friendship too. What all of these lessons have in common is that they are universal to all friendships and that they transcend time.

Lesson #1: Never Talk Behind Someone's Back

Gossip is gossip, even if we don't know if it is true. If you are about to say something about somebody and you have a single seed of doubt about whether it is true—it is gossip. To put it in legal terms, innocent until proven guilty. When we spread even the tiniest piece of gossip we are declaring ourselves the judge and jury and naming the person guilty of whatever it is we heard they might have done or said. It is irrelevant whether we are friends with the person or if we have no intention of ever befriending them.

When we spread gossip we are creating an identity as a person who wishes to hurt others by damaging their reputation. We are declaring to the world that we cannot be trusted as a friend, and all our friendships, present and future, will suffer because of it. This is a vicious, dangerous path to head down, because talking behind people's backs is a difficult behavior pattern to shake. The best solution is to put the brakes on now, or, as I will point out to my daughter, never start in the first place.

Lesson #2: Never Try to Change Your Friends

True friends respect one another for who they are. Again, this is similar to marriage advice. We cannot change other people to satisfy our own expectations of what we *think* they should be. Remember what made you want to be friends with this person in the first place. If the bond is genuine, those reasons will hold true and strengthen throughout the life of the friendship.

Similarly, it is important to value the friendship for what it is. Recognize what it is about the friendship that makes you feel close to that person, rather than looking for something that is not there. This goes back to seeing the reality of all your relationships, rather than comparing them to some impossible standard of perfection that does not exist.

Lesson #3: Don't Let Others Define Your Friendships

Make sure that you never forget who your true friends are and why you are friends, no matter what anybody tells you. Do not let other people's insecurities, gossip, or jealousy drive a wedge through the friendships you have worked so hard to develop. If you let other people interfere this way, then perhaps that is a sign that either your friendships need strengthening or they were never meant to be in the first place.

The only people who can define a friendship are the people in it. For instance, you know how often you need to be in contact with one another. I personally need to connect with some friends on a regular basis, while in other friendships, no matter how much time has passed, it's as if the conversation never stopped. Each friendship has its own parameters, and it is important that both members of the friendship understand each other's needs, limitations, and boundaries. As I said—in many ways, friendships are awfully similar to marriage.

Lesson #4: Don't Be Indifferent About Friendship

This lesson is inspired by a case on *Cristina's Court* that we called "Bridesmaid Blues." Before hearing this case, I always believed the biggest dramas surrounding the preparations leading up to a wedding involved the bride and groom and possibly some demanding relatives. Apparently I was wrong. The dramatic story that managed to monopolize and nearly hijack this wedding unfolded entirely between the bride and a bridesmaid.

These two women were friends who greatly trusted each other (or at least one of them thought so) and had been friends for long enough that one asked the other to be a bridesmaid in her upcoming wedding. This is a huge thing for one friend to ask another in any circumstance, but in this case it was even more of an honor. The bride did not have a lot of family and had only a total of three bridesmaids, so asking this friend obviously meant something to her. Generally agreed-upon etiquette in this situation says that if someone asks you to be a bridesmaid in her wedding and you don't feel up to the task for some reason, or feel that you are not a close enough friend to take on this role, you politely decline. If you accept, you are accepting all the responsibilities that come with such an important duty in one of the biggest events of a woman's life. Well, the bridesmaid in this situation accepted and the wedding preparations moved full speed ahead. But from the very start, it was obvious that "full speed ahead" was not the pace that this bridesmaid would be moving at.

From the get-go, the bridesmaid was either late or a complete no-show for all the wedding planning events. Feeling uneasy about this, the bride asked her friend if she really wanted to be a bridesmaid. Her friend told her yes, of course she did, and the show went on. It came to the day of the all-important bridal shower, a key event that all the bridesmaids traditionally plan together. This bridesmaid bailed on all her responsibilities and did not show up until the shower was almost over. But wait, there's more!

When it came time to order the bridesmaids' dresses, the bride made the task *extremely* easy for her bridal party. She told them all the style and color of dresses she preferred. And for the rogue bridesmaid who seemed unwilling to do anything, the bride even *ordered* the dress and the shoes for her. Literally all the bridesmaid had to do was call the store with her credit card. Guess whether that happened!

It was now the eleventh hour, or more specifically just one week before the wedding. It was too late for the bridesmaid to call with her credit card and buy the dress and shoes that the bride had picked out, and that the other two bridesmaids had successfully followed through on and purchased. So the rogue bridesmaid bought a ridiculous dress-and-shoe combo that did not match the rest of the bridal party at all. *Finally,* on the night of the rehearsal dinner, when this bridesmaid did not show up because she had to work, the bride came to her senses, recognized the reality of the situation, called the rogue bridesmaid, and asked her not to be a part of her wedding. She realized that this "friendship" was just not important to her. Cue the audience applause!

This wedding was nearly completely overshadowed by the selfish, self-entitled attitude of this bridesmaid—this "friend." She treated the entire responsibility of bridesmaid like just another deadline in her life (apparently she was not really good with deadlines—I know I wouldn't hire her). In fact the rogue bridesmaid sued her friend for reimbursement of the money spent on the dress and shoes. Meanwhile, the bride was miserable and the friendship was a long way past over. The bride thought she had made a close friend. The bridesmaid thought of it as just another obligation. Their friendship was a failed marriage of indifference.

When you are indifferent to the value of a friend, don't be surprised if one day that friend calls you and tells you not to bother showing up.

Lesson #5: Don't Use Friendship As a Weapon

My final friendship lesson is a very serious one with equally serious consequences for those who ignore its importance. As I alluded to earlier, kids today are much more sophisticated than they were twenty years ago. They are much more in tune with what is going on in society because of the Internet, texting, iPods, and such technological miracles that keep us constantly plugged into the rest of the world. Everything is public these days, and, in a way, that places friendships on a global-technology scale. This also means that the dark side of friendship—gossip, peer pressure, bullying, and ganging up on someone who looks or acts different—also plays out on a much larger scale.

I remember reading a news story a few years ago about a mom who decided to play what she would later refer to as a joke on her daughter's former friend, who she believed was spreading rumors about her daughter. The "joke," however, would ultimately lead to that teenage girl hanging herself and the mom being prosecuted for violating an Internet antihacking law. Do these sound like two unrelated events? Here's how they connected. Posing as a sixteen-year-old boy, the mom created an Internet social networking account and, through that Web site, befriended the teenage girl, earning her trust. Then, after some time, the "guy" from the social networking Web site turned against the teenage girl, showering her with cruel personal insults until she apparently broke down. The girl was later found dead, hanging in her closet.

The mom was eventually found guilty by a jury on three misdemeanors related to unauthorized Internet access (violating the Web site's user agreement). She was later acquitted by a judge, but unfortunately that does not change the impact. The story ends the same way.

This case of "cyberbullying" is a revealing glimpse into the grand technological scale that friendships and friendships gone bad play out on. It also showcases the role of the Internet in modern friendships.

Surfing the Internet and having conversations on these types of social Web sites can be very isolating as compared to live, human interaction. Staring into the glowing screen late at night, communicating with pictures and text versus people, can make those in an already vulnerable age-group feel even more alone and subject to the will of others. In the teenage girl's case, it made her a target for a vindictive adult who should have known better.

Look at the desire for revenge that pervaded this woman's better judgment and rationality. Look at how far she went just to get back at her daughter's "friend." Ultimately, she wanted to test the girl to see if she was her daughter's true friend. Her test cost the girl her life. This is not the friendship message we should be teaching our kids or one another. There is no room in a friendship for demeaning, bullying, blackmailing, or threatening behavior.

The Gift of Friendship

It is so important to make time for your friendships. After all, our friendships rejuvenate us! When you make time to be with your friends, you know it will be a time when you can let all pretenses down, be yourself, and, in the process, recharge your identity and revive your spirit as a woman. You are with a group of people whom you know, you trust, and you value. You make time for your friends because friendship is such an empowering, great "vacation" for smart, successful women to treasure. Sometimes we forget how much simply being around one another and being in communication enhances the smartest, sexiest pieces of our identity.

It has been wonderful to be able to reach out to my close girl-friends to share the news that I would be writing a book about women, for women, and that I would value their input greatly. They came through with flying colors and provided incredible, funny, witty observations about themselves and life in general. This was a great reminder to me of why I became friends with them in the first place. All of their qualities—from intelligence and humor to deep insight, warmth, and candid observations—came shining through. It is during times like this that the bonds of my friendships are reinforced and my love for my friends multiplies.

Why, then, do we forget this so often? It is easy to forget how valuable our friends are in good times versus relying on them only during bad times, when we need a shoulder to cry on.

Therefore, the most important, all-encompassing lesson that I will instill in my daughter is that friendship is a gift to be honored, respected, and constantly invested in.

My Verdict

Once upon a time there was a group of Dukes who made their friends into family and kept that family together, even after the Duke named Pee Wee passed on. The story of the Dukes shows that friendship is a valuable gift that is not freely given, should never be taken for granted, and, for the lucky ones—lasts for a lifetime.

"In her own words"

I asked some smart, confident women to share their thoughts on the laws covered in this chapter. Here is what they said, along with my responses.

Who do you think are better friends—men or women?

1. "I think that women are better friends, but that journey to good friendship is long and hard. Guys seem to make friends with each other more easily, but maybe the friendships lack the depth that female friendships have. With women you have to go on many 'friendship dates' before you can even call yourself acquaintances. You have to be a lot like them, or be the women they admire without making them feel jealous of you, in order to earn their approval. It's a tricky balance."

CP: She makes an interesting point toward the end, about earning the approval of other women. This is very true through your mid-thirties. As women get older they care less about what their friends do for a living and other external factors like that. Jealousy is based on factors like accomplishment and money rather than on a woman's true identity. As we get older we see other women for who they truly are and it's easier to be friends.

2. "Usually women, or men who are in secure relationships with nice women, are better friends. Women understand where I'm coming from, and men in friendships with women, because they have clearly figured out how to communicate with women as a species."

CP: I disagree, because the more that we understand the value of friendship, the less chance there is of lines being crossed.

186

3. "I think women are more skilled at developing and maintaining multiple deep friendships with other women and with men."

CP: This is because it is in women's nature to form deep connections. It is the nurturing part of ourselves.

4. "I think men make better friends to women, because I have known more women to end up falling for a male friend than vice versa. Men seem better at keeping it platonic."

CP: I think we get a bad rap in this sense. I have lots of guy friends but I never once thought of crossing that line, because I understand the value of a friendship. When you're older, you know that things like "friends with benefits" do not exist. Because there is no reason to risk a *true* friendship that way.

5. "It's a toss-up. On one hand, women fiercely defend our friends and those we love. On the other, we have a way of relentlessly holding grudges against enemies. Although we forgive what sometimes should be unforgivable, we never forget."

CP: We are strong while also being notoriously emotional. I guess this is why we women have such incredibly powerful intuition. These qualities give us a good sense of someone else's character.

PART IV
Identifying with Life

CHAPTER 8

Law #8: *Master the Balancing Act*

While I was preparing material for this book, the subject of Wonder Woman came up in a phone conversation I was having with a girlfriend. She and I were discussing the timeless idea that women are expected to have the ability to do it all. We were going back and forth on exactly what the phrase *it all* really means. Because if you looked at an assortment of pop-culture stereotypes, various bumper-sticker and refrigerator-magnet sayings, and the expectations often put on women, you really would think we are expected to be capable of clanking our magic wrist bracelets together and restoring world peace. Not to mention working a twelve-hour day, coming home and putting together an elaborate, tasty meal, cleaning the house, being a scholastic expert in every academic area for our children's homework, and being a sexy, attentive, charming, and vivacious wife around the clock. My friend and I were discussing where this societal perception came from and, more important, how we could set the record straight to save the sanity of overextended women everywhere. We were at an impasse.

Just as my girlfriend and I were ranting about how much we resented Wonder Woman and every superhero woman like her for reinforcing the superhuman-woman stereotype, my daughter, Sofia, walked into the room. I think all the Wonder Woman references must have piqued her interest, and she wanted to see if Mommy was now writing a comic book. She heard my end of the phone conversation, astutely picked up that we were discussing just how wonderful Wonder Woman was, and my perceptive little girl made the following comment: "But, Mommy, Wonder Woman doesn't have any kids!" If that is not the statement that instantly said it all I don't know what is.

Of course, Wonder Woman and all the superhuman women like her have no kids! I'm pretty sure they also do not have husbands, a house that does not magically self-clean, and other real-life obligations. How else would they have all that time to save the world? And please, let's get real for a minute—an invisible plane? Most women I know fantasize about wanting to disappear from the rest of the world—not be plainly visible to anyone who needs us for something. Our lives are not made to be magical or superhuman. I think our superpower is that we can manage the details of what, from the outside, appear to be ordinary lives, doing what needs to be done for our loved ones, and doing it in an extraordinary way.

Yet so many women fall into the trap and believe that they should somehow be superhuman and be everything to everyone or else they are failures as women. They buy into the folklore that all the other women (usually meaning fictional characters on television and in movies) are raising kids, being good wives, being the sixty-hour-per-week workplace superstar, waking up at dawn to dutifully go to the gym, keeping the house immaculate, and writing the great American novel in their spare time. And they're doing it without breaking a sweat, with an unwavering smile and never feeling stressed. Are you kidding me?

This woman is not a superhero—she's a figment of imagination! This is a dangerous piece of fiction that we all need to close the book on immediately, before we drive ourselves crazy competing with a woman who does not exist and never will.

The idea of seamlessly and constantly being all things to all people is a myth. But this does not mean that we cannot be our own version of a superwoman. It just depends on what qualities are your own equivalent of leaping tall buildings in a single bound, and incorporating them into your identity. For some women it is working and raising a happy family. For others it is being a stay-at-home mom. For still others it is about having a successful career and finding time to see the world. There is no universal superwoman identity. It is up to you to find the things that are most important to you and find a way to balance them in your life. At the end of the day you define what is most important to you.

I call this the balancing act of life. As individual women, we each balance so many countless hats and roles in life. Notice how, when a woman changes hats, among personal, political, professional, and otherwise, the world tends to stand up and take notice. It is as if they're saying, "Oh, no, she's out of her box; get the net!" Yet when a man does the same thing, seamlessly shifting among his hats and roles in life, there is no marching band, ticker-tape parade, or fireworks. He is simply applauded for being versatile. He is a renaissance man. That is part of the reason why I apply the term *balancing act* primarily to women. We are not only expected to gracefully balance all our different roles in life, but also expected, like master magicians, to do it invisibly and effortlessly.

If I tried to cover every single thing that every single woman on earth is tasked with balancing each day, this chapter would be a set of encyclopedias. So I have chosen the main ones, the most universal roles that most of us tackle from the moment we wake up in the morning until the blessed moment when our head finally hits the pillow at night. These are: balancing our traditional and contemporary roles, balancing responsibilities at work and at home, and the secret to mastering the entire balancing act.

Balancing Your Priorities

Yes, as the saying goes, we women have come a long way, baby. We have gone from Mrs. Cleaver to CEOs and Supreme Court justices in a relatively short period of time. With the feminist movement came a new world of infinite possibilities and a new frontier of personal and professional dreams that we could now aspire to that our mothers and grandmothers could not. However, as a lawyer and a businesswoman I will tell you that no good deal comes without a catch.

For most women, the catch when it came to feminism was that we were not *replacing* our traditional roles as wife, mother, caretaker of the home, and matriarch of the family. We were *adding* to those roles with new and exciting professional hats. One of the best visualizations I can think of for the donning of all these new hats was the opening sequence to *The Mary Tyler Moore Show*, when Mary jubilantly tossed her hat up into the air over the city streets where she had just landed her dream job. But, as my daughter Sofia would observe, "Mommy, Mary Richards didn't have any kids!"

That does not mean that Mary Richards, with her career ambitions, had less of a balancing act to juggle than the rest of us. But the reality is that for most women, the concept of feminism meant adding new responsibilities to old ones and finding a way to make it all work.

Many women seem to have interpreted this as being required to abandon traditional wifely "duties" such as making dinner for one's husband, taking the lead role in child rearing, and keeping a pleasant, welcoming home. They feel that since the feminist movement freed them of being locked into these roles, if they perform the roles, they are somehow going backward or defeating the entire purpose of feminism. They feel like they have to suddenly prove something as contemporary, feminist women, and that if they put on an apron and make cookies—even if they really *want* to—it would be an affront to women everywhere and silent confirmation that women are indeed weaker than men.

Honestly, I have never understood this thinking, and on top of that, I vehemently disagree with it. I believe in and defend the power of a woman, her character and strength, and the fact that anyone should be judged on that alone. But we are not doing ourselves any favors as women by denying a part of our identity that most of us happen to cherish and nurture. For this reason, I call myself a "confused feminist." As I mentioned earlier in the book, a confused feminist is able to choose what she wants to do in life. My unofficial definition of this term is someone who wants it all in the workplace, at home, and anywhere else. I define it in my life as doing everything in my power to maintain a successful career without holding anything back. And at the end of the day, I enjoy coming home and cooking dinner for my husband (and sometimes he even reciprocates) and being the best mother to Sofia that she could ever wish for. I also do not consider it a betrayal of feminism if I enjoy being taken care of by my husband sometimes. I allow myself to be the boss at work and the coddled woman at home. I feel treasured and feminine when my husband opens doors for me or picks up the check. I know that he does not do things for me because he thinks that I am incapable of doing them for myself. He respects all the hats I wear in life and sees them all as unique expressions of who I am as a person and as his wife. Wearing the traditional hat of a woman is not demeaning to feminism—it is empowering to women.

It's funny how perceptions and attitudes on this subject have changed and ultimately come around full circle through the years. Once the feminist movement came along, the old-school values of

Leave It to Beaver were quickly discarded—out with the old and in with the new. And now, many women are embracing their traditional roots and leaving their professions to become stay-at-home moms. Others are balancing their family life while still embracing what used to be thought of as the feminist role of a professional. Of course, now, balancing a career and family is not exactly cutting-edge or even feminist. It is called being a woman and doing what needs to be done.

When feminism became all the rage, it seemed that many women quickly discarded their prior roles as housewives and moms without a second thought. They did not want to accidentally get left behind in the pages of women's history. And then history cycled around, showing us all how to balance the best of both worlds.

The lesson is, don't be so quick to discard what comes naturally— what *you* actually want out of life—just because you do not necessarily see yourself reflected in current events. The only current events you need to worry about are the ones in your life. Stay true to your identity and never let it be said that you are doing something wrong or that your life is outdated compared to what the rest of the world is doing. There is no wrong way of being true to yourself. And remember, what goes around comes around.

I do not consider it a contradiction at all to prioritize both sets of hats in my life—traditional and contemporary. These are all aspects of my complete identity as a woman. I would no more deny my role as nurturer to my family than I would my role as legal advocate. They are all a part of who I am.

I think I am only slightly exaggerating when I say that it is our ability to balance all our roles with grace while staying true to ourselves that should make women the most revered creatures on the planet! If aliens from another planet observed how things work here on Earth, who do you think they would presume holds most of the power? Women are central, calming, unifying figures everywhere we go, from the office to home. Without women, it is possible that men would be too busy looking for lost keys and wallets to get anything else done. I say this as I think of my gorgeous and brilliant husband. My father, the astutely observant, successful surgeon, husband, and father, has always referred to the role of wife and mother as the hardest job in the world. He says that this is why women are so valuable, because what would men do without them?

Now combine Mrs. Cleaver and Mary Richards and tell me that the woman who makes this work is not a superhero in her own right. The reason for the "women and children first" rule of lifeboats and in other disasters may possibly be because we are far too valuable for the human race to live without. The smart men want to make sure that if worse comes to worst, at least some of us will survive. And you know the ones who do survive will quietly pick up the slack left by the women who didn't make it and carry on.

For these reasons and more, it is amazing to me that people can still utter the phrase *just a woman* with a straight face. This is particularly unjustified when applied to stay-at-home moms. Women who wear the hats of mother and spouse twenty-four/seven have the most important job in the world while also experiencing the best rewards— the opportunity to completely shape the lives of their children and husband, without interruption. This is a tremendous gift, but also an enormous responsibility to undertake.

Whether you work inside the home or outside the home, it is still work, and you deserve full credit for it. If anyone does not believe you, I suggest you challenge them to trade places for a week and then let them see what "just a housewife" or "just a stay-at-home mom" is really all about. As the saying goes, don't judge someone else until you walk a mile in their shoes—or, in this case, sandals.

Whether you are a confused feminist, a stay-at-home mom, or all the other descriptions women use in defining how we balance our roles in life, it is essential that *you* set your own priorities. Never let anyone else tell you what is most important to you in life, and certainly never let anyone make you feel as if you have to apologize for any of the hats you wear.

This also means that we should never feel as if we have to overcompensate, especially to prove that as women we are not weak. We are far too busy managing our responsibilities to be weak! Most women cannot even schedule a sick day into their schedule, no matter how sick they are. Whoever first called us weak was clearly trying to build a case of some sort for himself.

Women who believe that they are weak or inferior in any way are in danger of hitting the overcompensation warpath. You know the one I mean: "I am woman; hear me roar—now get out of my way, if you know what's good for you!" I experienced this as a female attorney still trying to prove myself in a man's world. I was hell-bent on proving, without a shadow of a doubt, that anything the men could do, I could do better.

My quest hit its peak when I became pregnant with Sofia. I had never felt more beautiful, together, secure, happy, and confident about myself. Here I was feeling the most feminine and womanly that I had ever felt in my life, yet I felt that being pregnant was a big (and growing daily) reminder to all the men in my life that I was a woman. I was surprised that I was feeling this way, especially at the age of thirty-five, because I *was* so secure with myself by that age. I was very careful, especially at work and around men, not to make a show of my pregnancy. I would do things like sit behind a desk (or my bench) so they would not see my pregnant belly. I was determined to work twice as hard, proving that I was not weak just because I was pregnant. In my mind I did not want to give people a reason to doubt my abilities or judge me in any way. I had been a professional for so long, and I had this idea in my head that being pregnant would somehow affect my brain cells. Nobody treated me differently, but I did not want to give them a reason to.

In ancient cultures pregnant women were revered, worshipped, and pampered as goddesses who were tasked with bringing a beautiful new life into the world. And here I was rushing around the office like a crazy person fighting a battle—except the only person I was fighting was myself. What I would not have given for a big, cushy pillow to lounge on while people fed me grapes and fanned me with giant feathers. Ah, the good old days before Rome fell.

My "battle" phase lasted even beyond my pregnancy. I wanted to make sure that if any of my male coworkers had any lingering recollections of me in my "weakened" state, I would erase those memories by making them see me as a professional first and a woman second. Well, as it turned out, I was driving myself crazy for nothing. No man cared that I was pregnant (except my husband—for good reason). My paranoia that I was seen by men as somehow weaker was all in my head. All of my male buddies treated me the same before, during, and after my pregnancy. I must have had a momentary lapse of sanity. Then and now, most people associate me with my professional hats first anyway. This is not because they don't respect my roles as wife and mother. It is simply that most people know me that way in my public life.

I, on the other hand, cherish my private roles as wife and mother above anything else in life—no competition. Connecting with and taking pride in the most natural parts of being a woman, as a caretaker and nurturer, does not take away from or weaken my professional roles. In fact, I think the loving support and strength that come from my husband and daughter make me a stronger woman and more perceptive in *all* aspects of my life, professional included.

My family is my greatest source of strength, and they make prioritizing my life a simple task. It has been this way for me ever since I was little and my parents and siblings were my family and therefore my top priority. My parents in particular inspired me to become a strong woman in all areas of my life, without boundaries. They treated my sister and me as equals to my brother and told us to do what we wanted to do in life, to be happy in doing it, and never to use being female as an excuse for anything less than greatness. My father is an extremely traditional, old-fashioned man, but in that way he inspired my "confused feminist" roots. He taught me that both genders are equal in value and also in the roles we play in life. My parents also looked to the women who shared this attitude before me when shaping their expectations of me. Inspired by the first female doctor in America, Elizabeth Blackwell, and also by my father, my first dream was of being a doctor. I remember sharing my dream with my mother and her telling me that yes, of course I could be a doctor, because there were already so many women who were doctors. I am glad that there are so many strong women who paved the way for the rest of us to take our identities in whichever direction we want. I also hope that my Sofia and all the other future women of her generation are inspired to take on more roles than ever before.

I think the ultimate definition of a feminist, confused or otherwise, is a woman who is ready and willing to take on this responsibility of paving new roads. It takes a great deal of strength to retain the things we love the most about being women while also taking on new roles in the business world, political arena, or world stage. Feminism, to me, is removing any barriers that keep you from doing what you want in life. If that means being a stay-at-home mom and finding absolute joy and fulfillment in taking care of your family, then yes, you are a feminist, because you and no one else made that decision. If that means taking the world by storm and aspiring to greater levels of leadership than any other woman before you, that is also the definition of a feminist, because you and nobody else made that decision. But for most of us, being a feminist simply means balancing all our roles in life, keeping our personal priorities straight, and finding happiness and fulfillment in each hat we wear as women.

Balancing Your Career

Balancing a career is an entire balancing act in itself. When you go to work each morning you are entering a new world with a new cast of characters outside of your home life, and each with a new set of demands and career challenges. For most of us this means that by the time we finally get our family up, out of bed, fed, and ready for their day, we get to go to the office, where a whole new set of responsibilities awaits. We can really be the ultimate masochists—in marriage, our personal life, and our careers!

Our male counterparts have a similar level of responsibility to ours, as far as work goes, yet they appear to manage it with the grace of true sadists. Men figured out a long time ago that work is work; it is not going anywhere, so why beat yourself up when you want to take a break from it?

My husband is the all-time supreme example of this attitude, and also of how to confront a common career challenge that women face—multitasking. Christopher is a dedicated and brilliant lawyer, but when he is not working his mind is nowhere near the office. In fact—and as you may have ascertained from my stories so far—when Christopher is not working he can almost always be found hitting the links. I am astounded at and just a little bit jealous of how he can schedule a golf day during the week (typically every Friday, but sometimes more) and completely push his work from his mind without even one backward glance. I, on the other hand, am launched into a gigantic guilt trip if I take one hour during the day to get my nails done.

This kind of thinking and unnecessary self-torture make me wonder how masochistic we women need to get before we realize that nobody is judging us except ourselves. So I don't do this anymore. Working against us is the fact that as women we seem to be biologically programmed to do more than one thing at once. This also translates into thinking about several other things at once, in addition to the thing we are supposed to be focused on. For example, if I were the one playing golf on a Friday, I guarantee that I would be reviewing a different case in my head with each new hole.

Similar to how a little perfectionism is a virtue, but a runaway case of perfectionism can be the end of us, this kind of multitasking can also be a double-edged sword. When managed correctly, multitasking can make us productive, proactive, and forward-thinking. But when you lose control of your capability to multitask, it can send you scattered in a million different directions with not a single task completed in any direction. This, in turn, makes every task go from molehill to mountain in an instant while simultaneously sending your stress level through the roof. This is not helpful in any work environment.

The solution is to learn to focus on one task at a time and compartmentalize. By that, I mean to bring what you *should* be working on and focusing on to the front of your mind and imagine all those other pesky thoughts floating away to the sidelines. If it makes you feel better, tell yourself that you are not discarding or ignoring important thoughts or tasks. You're just giving them a coffee break until the work at hand has been completed. At the beginning of each day I make a list of the things I want to accomplish and then I prioritize that list throughout the day as new situations present themselves. As long as I get through at least some of the things at the top of that list, it is okay.

By training yourself to approach and attack tasks with this laser focus, you are likely to get better results from your work in a shorter period of time. The purpose of genuine multitasking is to balance your workload in a way that gets the work done efficiently. Allowing your attention to get scattered and your stress level to go through the roof is the exact opposite of balance. Everyone has their own way of multitasking and managing—you just have to find yours.

When balancing their careers, many women also confront the infamous corporate ladder. Early in my professional life, I learned to take phrases like *corporate ladder* and other cleverly worded career clichés with a grain of salt. After all, most were invented by people whose job it was to create such catchphrases to motivate the masses.

I have always preferred to gain my inspiration and motivation from my parents and, eventually, the part of my identity that has evolved through years of hard work in my profession. My parents made it clear to me that the only glass ceiling I would ever need to bust through to succeed was the one I set for myself.

My parents taught me to set my own goals and my own expectations, and develop a work ethic to live up to my own standards. The way that I would gauge my success would be through the knowledge that I was true to myself and my passion (the law); I never strayed outside the boundaries of my work ethics and the ethics of my profession; and, most important, I felt a sense of pride and happiness as a result of my career. The pride and knowledge that I have earned whatever success I have experienced, through a lot of hard work and perseverance, have propelled me forward and helped me face and conquer a variety of challenges in my career.

Anyone working her way up through a profession faces a multitude of challenges and obstacles. This is par for the course, since anything worth having is worth working for. I learned from my parents the importance of *earning* success.

A long time ago I stopped thinking of myself as a woman professional or a female lawyer. I think of myself simply as a professional, because results are what people remember. Gender is secondary. If your work is better than anyone else's, who do you think they're going to recognize? This is a big lesson for women, because this type of irrational fear is one of our downfalls. If we ignore the perception that a woman's work is somehow of lesser value than a man's, everyone else will too.

I realized this downfall during my first court case. I was trying to ask the smartest questions and trying hard to have the best insights. I learned that if I did not have a connection with myself and was not connected to the case at hand, I could never do justice to the case at hand. How could I assist in resolving a problem when I did not understand it on a human level? Once I realized that, I was able to proceed with the case as a professional without feeling the need to "outlawyer" anyone in the process.

One of my girlfriends from law school is a sexy, gorgeous, and tiny Filipina woman. What her adversaries do not immediately realize, but quickly learn, is that her intelligence surpasses her physical appearance by leaps and bounds. She decided long ago, as a newly graduated lawyer, that she would go into private practice. This tiny, sexy dynamo has been up against some of the biggest corporate giants and major brands on the planet and has always won. Her soft confidence and femininity can be misperceived as signs of weakness rather than strength. This can cause her professional competitors to underestimate her. Because once she opens her mouth, she is ruthless. She does not see herself as a weaker woman professional, and she certainly never looked for any free ride. She has aggressively pursued and earned every bit of her success with intelligence and an unassailable work ethic.

As a woman trying to earn respect, remember that soft confidence sometimes speaks volumes louder than trying to scream your way to the top. It is most important as a professional to allow your work to be the measuring stick of your worth. Good work and professionalism are genderless. I learned this from my first boss and also from my father. Stop fighting imaginary battles, like the one I fought with myself while pregnant, believing that people see you as the weaker sex in the workplace.

Working Your Way Up

There is no such thing as a free ride in any profession, and to feel entitled about what you deserve is an insult to all the people in your profession before you who paved your way through their own hard work and determination to succeed. You cannot expect to graduate from school and step directly into your dream job without paying your dues first. You have to work your way up. Even if you are inwardly confident that you can handle any job or task, you have to prove it first. Despite what you may think, your supervisors and colleagues are not psychic, no matter how glowing your résumé is.

At the beginning of any new career (this includes a career transition later in life), you may have to work harder than your colleagues to prove yourself. This has nothing to do with being a woman either. My father had to work extra hard to prove his skills and ability as a surgeon when he first moved to the United States, simply because he was an immigrant. Everyone faces their own obstacles at work, and those who look for shortcuts are only shortchanging themselves and the future of their career.

I know that there are always going to be challenges in my career and in life, but I have no doubt that I will be able to face them. It is my privilege to do all the things that are asked of me, and being fortunate enough to be successful in my career has reinforced that lesson.

What I have also gained as a result of my career is the ability to balance, especially among all the hats I wear as a professional woman. Years ago, as I was just entering the workforce, if you would have listed all the different things I now do as parts of my career, and asked me if I would be able to do them all, I would have told you that you were crazy! I realize that on paper my life looks absolutely overwhelming. I always knew I wanted a successful career, but I just had no idea what it would entail. And yet now here I am doing it every day, in the eye of the storm, so to speak. Now that I am doing it, balancing my hectic life is suddenly manageable and fun. This is because I love and have passion for everything I do and I am good at it. I take on what I can handle because I am capable of it.

From the very beginning of my career all the way to the present, there has been another extremely valuable lesson I have learned about how to achieve success and happiness on the job: The most important thing you can bring with you to work every day . . . is you. Whether your career is your passion or if it is how you support your family and provide a future for your children, you wear your distinctive identity in every aspect of your job.

I learned from my first job that bringing my own unique identity into the workplace was a key to my success. My identity is what makes it possible to connect with my clients and litigants—everyday people from every walk of life—and help them through their problems. Embracing my identity has always been the most important way of allowing myself to be of service in my profession and in all my roles in life.

For all the time I have spent in the workplace over the years, I have always been one hundred percent Cristina, because I don't know how to be anyone else. I think that this courage to be myself, under all circumstances and in all situations, has a lot to do with the success and happiness I have achieved throughout my career. I have talked about the example set by my father as a role model and guide in all aspects of my life. I attribute so much of my success in all areas of my life to following his blueprint of what success is.

It is important to discover a similar level of personal motivation and inspiration in your life. Because there are some things that all the corporate motivation courses, legal textbooks, and business education cannot give you. Who you are as a person tops that list. There is nobody else in the world who can bring what you bring to your job and your profession. *That* is your biggest career asset, because it comes through in everything you do from the moment you arrive at work until the moment you change hats and leave for home at night. And when you turn the light off, be comfortable with who you are and trust yourself.

Mastering the Balancing Act

Nothing comes easy in life, and the daily effort it takes to balance all your roles, from career woman to wife, mother, and member of your community, is proof positive of this. Mastering the balancing act is in our blood as women, usually bred in us by our amazing, multitasking mothers. My mother is the perfect example of that. She has always managed to place the needs of her family first, while also keeping our home in perfect order, raising and educating three children, working outside the home, and remaining the backbone of our family the whole time, through whatever challenges and turmoil we face (as all families do). She created a safe and balanced family atmosphere for us.

My mother has an uncanny way of balancing several different tasks at the same time without ever revealing the skillful juggling act in progress. As much as I try to follow her example, I get the feeling that every once in a while I let on that it is not as easy as it looks. Then I reassure myself that nobody is perfect and that, as much as I try, I will most likely never be as skilled as my mother at mastering life's balancing act.

Nevertheless, there are some things I have learned from juggling the ridiculous number of roles in my life that I voluntarily and happily take on. No, I am not crazy, and I certainly know how to say no when a *firm* no is needed. I take on all these roles in life because my mother taught me that I can do it. I learned from her that no matter how much is demanded of me, there is nothing I cannot handle. The biggest strength and lesson I have learned through it all is to approach every role and responsibility I have in life from the perspective of privilege.

If you approach your life with this perspective, then balancing all your roles will not be a chore. They will come as naturally to you as the day you first accepted them. Go back to your first day of work at an exciting new job, the day you got married, or the moment you gave birth to your child. Remember the excitement you felt about this new and exciting role in your life. You may have felt as if anything were possible. You understood that there would eventually be challenges, but had no doubt that you would be able to face them.

That is the key to managing the balancing act. So the next time you find yourself stressed out at the end of another taxing day, when once again there are not enough hours in the day and everyone needs you at once; your child has ten places to be dropped off at and picked up from; your boss needs you to stay after work; your community board has called a last-minute meeting; *and* your husband has invited his friends for an impromptu dinner that he volunteered you to cook, remember—you can do this. You were born to do this; you have it in your blood to do this and to do it well!

I would hope that someday my daughter will say about me, "My mother is my mother, but she was this incredible go-getter, she fought and stood up for what she believed in, and she worked extremely hard, but she was always my mother." I want her to know that being true to yourself and being true to each of the roles you play in life is the key to success and happiness.

I want her (and you) to take pride in every hat she wears in life, knowing that the only reason these demands are being placed on her is because there is nobody else on this planet who can do any of these things as well as she can. In this way, a balancing act is not a burden—it is a blessing.

My Verdict

Even Wonder Woman would find it challenging to balance all the roles, responsibilities, and priorities that we real-life women face in our lives. Fortunately, instead of magic wristbands and an invisible plane, we have strength of spirit and the knowledge in our hearts that *we can do it*.

"IN HER OWN WORDS"

I asked some smart, confident women to share their thoughts on the laws covered in this chapter. Here is what they said, along with my responses.

How do you balance your different life roles?

1. "Since I am a stay-at-home mom, it's hard work having to take care of my kids and their needs, while still showing them love and attention, and then making time for my husband as well. Sometimes I'd like to clone myself, or be an octopus. It's just about figuring out our own way of doing things and how to juggle. It's not just about how you will be able to do it—you simply must find a way. We all have our own methods. There is no perfect way of doing it."

CP: Being a stay-at-home mom is the hardest job in life and the hardest balancing act. She says there is no secret formula, and she's right. It goes back to loving what you do and seeing every responsibility you have as a privilege.

2. "Nobody knows what I go through unless they also have a child with a disability or autism, like my son has. I think my children will remember me for everything—being there for them, keeping up with the house, being strict, along with love and attention. All I can do is try my best to do it all, and that's what we all should do. There is no such thing as doing it all, but we can try. The impossible is possible."

CP: We should all stand up and listen to this woman saying that the impossible is possible. She's right that few of us can understand what she goes through. What an inspiration to all of us!

Continued

3. "There is no such thing as a work-life balance. Something's always got to give, and usually it's your sanity. I have a demanding job and two little kids. My family comes first. If one of my kids is sick I am going to be there for them even if I have an important deadline. Sometimes what suffers is the laundry, the dishes, and my unshaven legs. But do I want my kids to sit around at my funeral remembering how downy soft their underwear was, how they could see themselves in the dishes, and how smooth and silky Mommy's legs were? Nope. I would be thrilled with a headstone reading, *Here lies our beloved mom. She held us while we puked.*"

CP: Now, *that's* prioritizing! This is a woman who sees through stereotypes and says, "I don't care what anyone else thinks." She is wearing her identity as a mom first, without making any excuses, while still balancing her other roles with a great, smart, honest perspective we could all learn from.

4. "As women, we can multitask and conquer so many projects at the same time while always putting family first. Our downfall while doing this, however, is allowing ourselves to carry the world on our shoulders."

CP: It is a careful balance. But it's important to know your limitations and what you can or cannot do.

Chapter 9

Law #9: *Reinvent Yourself*

W hen I was offered the opportunity to work in television, I knew I could not say no, because of the experience it would be. I knew virtually nothing about this new industry called Hollywood that I was being asked to leap into. My woman's sixth sense let me know that I was being faced with a moment to reinvent myself in a new career role. I could take the chance that life was offering me and redefine myself, especially while dealing with something I already loved: the law.

It was one of those moments in life when you take stock of who you are, what you want, where you are in your life, and what you feel ready to accept. I took inventory and realized that, yes, I was prepared to reinvent myself and recommit myself to a new career. I felt a calling for this new career in which I knew I would have to challenge myself and find my place all over again, just as I had done previously. I knew it would not be easy, and that it would be a completely different life from the life I was used to. But I was ready. . . . Lights, camera, action!

The Art of Reinvention

If necessity is the mother of invention, then how does a woman know when it is time to *re*invent herself? This is not something that we are alerted to, as if by an alarm clock or calendar. Reinventing yourself is not a requirement, and some women have extremely satisfying, fulfilling lives full of passion without ever feeling the urge to redefine themselves.

To clarify, the art of reinvention does not mean that we are changing who we are as women or somehow negating our identities. It means that we are reestablishing new priorities, goals, careers, or paths for ourselves. In order to do this, we need to be on solid, secure ground as to who we are and what we want out of life.

Madonna seems to make reinvention work seamlessly about every five years or so. She apparently has no doubt at all about who she is as a person; therefore she has the security and self-confidence to change various things about herself and her life when she feels ready. This is not reinvention by committee or by popular opinion. When she wants to change something, she does not second-guess herself. She is a great current role model for reinventing yourself on your own terms.

Reinvention goes hand in hand with self-development. We cannot develop ourselves if we do not know who we are. We need to know who we are, what we stand for, what we are all about, what we want from life, and the kind of person we are. Fortunately, this entire book has been a lesson in how to develop yourself in all areas of life, from your strength of individual identity to your willingness to take risks and how to succeed in your relationships with others. When you develop yourself, you are developing your strengths and, in due course, your identity. Once you have mastered these laws, you will have developed a strong sense of who you are and you will have learned to trust your instincts. You will have created firm roots into the ground, and you will not move unless you decide to move.

This means you will have developed to a stage where you know who you are. Because once you know who you are it is easy to reinvent, improve, or take risks in any of the roles you play in life or any aspect of your life that you choose to change. This could mean a career change, a cross-country move, making the decision to go out at night with friends more often, or going out and getting a brand-new look because you feel it is what you want and this is the time to do it. As women we have so many different career options and possible paths in life. We have all the potential in the world to follow any of those paths. Reinvention is choosing the one that works for you right now, based on what is going on with the rest of your life.

Life has a way of throwing experiences at you that you learn and grow from. I was able to make the decision to perform in the ACME comedy show for these reasons and more. I was at a point in my life where I needed a new direction—an entirely new experience completely out of the box from what I was used to in the comfort zone I had developed for myself. I was stable with who I am and what I am ready to undertake, and that gave me the willingness to take the risk.

Take your own life inventory when the opportunity to reinvent yourself in some way comes along. Look at what life is offering you and decide whether you want to do it or let the opportunity for self-development pass you by. Reinvention is about not being afraid to do something because you are secure with who you are in life.

I have a friend who is a terrific example of how to reinvent yourself when you know the time is right. This is a woman who has really accomplished it all in her career, managing money. She did this by working her butt off from the moment she hit the ground running to the moment when she realized that she had moved all the way up in her profession and achieved all her goals. With this realization, this woman also became conscious that the thrill of this particular role in her life had gone.

She took stock of her life and her passions and found that she was now passionate about kids and the idea of teaching. Her role as a mom strengthened this passion. She sought to find a way to satisfy her enthusiasm for working and her love of children, gained from being a mother. My friend decided to go back to school and get her master's degree in education and become a teacher.

This is an example of a woman who was in a positive, albeit restless place in her life, and she was extremely secure with her identity, strengths, talents, and ambitions. If you are going to make the decision to reinvent yourself, this is the place you should be working from.

Unfortunately, what appears to be the motivation to reinvent ourselves often shows up during the hard times in our lives, when the last thing we should be thinking about is change. If you are trying to reinvent yourself because you feel your life is somehow broken, and you feel that making drastic changes will somehow fix that—resist the temptation. Do not do it because you are trying to find strength in yourself or just because you feel obligated to take a risk. These are the wrong reasons for change.

A friend of mine tried to reinvent herself the wrong way, and fortunately she was able to realize her mistake before it was too late. She left a stable nursing career, feeling that this was not the job for her. That in itself might have turned out fine. But she was young and, as young people do, she felt a desire to go from one extreme to the other as a way of reinventing her identity. So she left for Los Angeles to reinvent herself as an actor. In her mind, that was the opposite of a career in nursing. In nursing, she once explained to me, you are encouraged to hide your emotions behind a poker face, while in acting you are encouraged to take a sledgehammer to any emotional walls built around you.

But she took the notion of making a major change so far that the former small-town girl soon found herself immersed in the danger-ously fast social scene of a big city. She took her reinvention to ex-tremes that compromised her health and safety. In a way, she was trying to put a Band-Aid on her frustration with nursing and with her inability to "find herself." Because she did not take the time to identify her real challenges and life issues, she tried to fix them the wrong way.

Fortunately, my friend's story has a happy ending. Thanks to an-other friend's help, she was able to pull herself out of her free fall and emerged with a clear head and clear picture about who she was. She was able to see how nursing, acting, and her other personal and profes-sional choices were all stepping-stones to her future decisions, and how they contributed to her new, stable identity. She ultimately found her-self by examining her triumphs and her mistakes, and through her willingness to confront the consequences of her choices.

In fact, my friend was so happy with her newfound clarity about life that she dyed her hair pink. Despite what many people thought, she did not do this as a form of rebellion or a way of acting out. I find it funny that, even after my friend would give an honest answer to the people who asked about her hair, they remained doubtful—as if she were holding back the real reason and was in quiet rebellion against the world. But she was not rebelling against anything, not anymore. This was simply her way of expressing on the outside how great she finally felt on the inside—nothing more and nothing less than that. She had found the strength from within to be herself and needed to express her joy.

My friend's story shows how, when you don't have a grip on your identity and then you intentionally make yourself as emotionally vul-nerable as possible, you are at the mercy of your circumstances. This is never a strong place to make life choices from.

During hard times, such as in times of personal weakness, or after personal tragedies, financial struggles, divorces, or breakups, the only responsibility you have toward yourself is to grieve, heal, take some time to get refocused on your life, and, in many cases, learn a life lesson. Any kind of change that you create from a place of sadness, fear, or desperation will not be for the better, and you will almost certainly regret it down the line.

You also need to make sure you are prepared with the right skills, knowledge, and resources before reinventing a whole area of your life. We heard a case on *Cristina's Court* of a woman who thought it would be a good idea to start her own business, a hair salon. She decided it would be smart to reinvent herself as a business owner. What was not smart was how she failed to research what it takes to successfully own and operate a business. What this woman lacked in common sense she tried to make up for with passion. But passion can take one only so far when there are bills to be paid, especially when one has apparently delegated to friends all the bill paying, expense reports, customer management, and virtually everything else that a business owner should have her fingers on.

The basis of the lawsuit was that this woman was suing one of her hairdressers for violation of contract, stating that the hairdresser took clients away from her. I asked her how many clients her hairdresser allegedly took away from her—she had no idea. In fact, I asked her how many clients she had—no idea. I asked her how much money she made—no idea. ("My friend handles that.") I asked her what her expenses were—no idea. I asked her about her utilities, finances, bills, operations—no idea. I finally asked her how she had come to the lump sum of money she was suing her friend for: She made it up.

I decided that this must be the worst businesswoman alive. She never should have gone into business in the first place—any business. I don't think I've ever met anyone else who didn't know how much they were paid. This woman should have developed herself more in the area of business before investing all this time and money in a new project like this, where other people's jobs were also affected. You should not just start a business because you are tired and bored in your life, unless you are prepared to handle the responsibility.

This is an example of a woman who tried to adjust the circumstances of her life in a way that she was clearly not prepared to handle, to change things on the surface without exploring her identity on the inside. Reinvent yourself from the inside out instead of the outside in. Figure out what defines you—the most important and unique parts of your identity that you are the most proud of, what makes you hold your head high as you strut down the street. Those are the qualities you need to hang on to. They make up your true essence.

Reinvent yourself for the right reasons, like the ones discussed in this book: to be a smarter woman, to make yourself feel stronger and sexier, to be more successful in friendships, to gain strength of identity, to maintain your marriage, to learn to speak up and take risks, along with improving all the other areas of your life that can benefit and flourish from the positive self-development that emerges from a positive place in your life. When you make life changes for the right reasons, reinvention can be a very powerful tool.

Self-development and reinvention are both tools that all mothers should pass on to their children, particularly, in the context of this book, their daughters. I encourage my daughter, Sofia, to develop herself by allowing her to be fearless and trust her instincts, within the boundaries of safety and reason, of course. And it seems to be working too—but it still makes me nervous sometimes. I am her mom, after all.

For instance, Sofia has always dived headfirst into every extracurricular activity, sport, and class that she has taken part in. From T-ball to dancing, gymnastics, and karate, she is the quintessential excited kid and eager participant. She has always counted the minutes between classes and practices and just about drags my husband and me into the car, for fear of being one second late.

So when we enrolled her in a swim class, going along with what we thought were her wishes, it was a complete surprise to us when she started crying during class and telling us how much she hated it. We thought swimming was a great skill for any kid to learn that would help her throughout life, and was therefore a good way to help Sofia develop herself. But she just continued to resist going to swimming class, even going so far as to become hysterical and start hyperventilating during class. We knew she was not being a brat, because honestly that is the last word I would ever use to describe my daughter. She is just not like that. And believe me, I am not one to baby, coddle, or give in to my daughter. I think we are actually harder on her because she is an only child.

It turned out that it was not the idea of swimming that was sending Sofia into fits and tantrums. She did not like the form of instruction. It was just too strong for her personality. The irony is that my husband and I have strong personalities, and so does our daughter. But, nevertheless, that method of swimming was way too aggressive for her and was making her fear swimming. We listened to her, honored her instincts, changed her class, and now she is a happy little fish in the water. This is also an example of all the lessons we are talking about in this book. Sofia did not have a fear of speaking up; I trusted my instincts in listening to her; and she was allowed to develop a big piece of her identity in the process.

Sofia's lack of hesitation to speak up and share her point of view demonstrates one of the many great lessons we can learn from children: Their gut instincts are like our womanly sixth sense. They are always honest and point us in the direction of where we need to go and toward the next step in developing our identities. Children are proof that we have always had this sixth sense, but the older we get, the more tainted we often become by society.

This situation was a great lesson in trusting our instincts, and her instinct was that she just did not want to learn how to swim the way that she was being taught. I had realized from the beginning, when

Sofia first started resisting, that my gut was telling me to pull her from the class. I stopped fighting my gut, along with my instinct as a mother to "be right" and "do what's best for her," because in this case, what was best for Sofia was letting her know how much we trusted her decisions.

It is important to instill this kind of self-confidence in your children so they will have the confidence to develop their identities. The younger they are, the more important it is to let them learn to trust themselves. I do not want to create doubt in Sofia about her ability to make decisions in her own mind. I want to show my daughter that as a woman she should have faith in her own opinion. I want to show her that her self-development is ultimately in her hands as she grows as a woman.

Instinct or not, as a parent it is my job to make sure that the decisions my daughter makes are in her best interests. But at the same time there are great lessons to be learned from a child about the purity of our gut instincts.

Finally, to answer the question I asked at the beginning of this section about the right time to reinvent yourself: Reinvention and self-development are in the hands of each individual woman who chooses to do it. You will know when the time is right when you are at a point in your life where you have no doubt as to who you are as a person, when you are ready to change and ready to accept the challenges. You will know when it is right because you will be doing it for nobody else but yourself.

Reinventing Yourself for Love

Enter the litigant on *Cristina's Court* who was so desperate to find somebody that she would try to change herself for each man she dated. She was a young girl, a single mom, and she was not emotionally secure or ready to be dating anyone, let alone reinventing herself for each new boyfriend. She just saw the man as the solution to her personal instability, without thinking of the consequences for her daughter, or of anything else. She could not see the forest for the trees, as the expression goes. So she made one bad decision after another, changing some part of herself for each new man until she finally met a man who immediately saw through her act, saw her insecurities, and used them to his advantage.

While she played the part of a good "wife," caring for this man's every whim and desire, all he was doing was using her and cheating on her during their two-and-a-half-year relationship. And she knew about it too! She would confirm his affairs by checking his phone and yet would never leave him, because she so desperately wanted to have somebody in her life—anybody. She also justified staying in the relationship, in that sometimes he could be kind, sweet, and helpful. So she continued to perform the role of someone she was not while he kept making mistakes and cheating on her.

But there was at least a small piece of this girl who just wasn't buying the act. And the way this part of her identity chose to express itself was through a raging temper. This girl may not have had the guts to tell this guy what she really thought of him, because it conflicted with the role of happy homemaker she was portraying. However, the guy must have known that something was amiss when he came home to find his Xbox smashed, along with the windshield of his car (there's that passive-aggressive downfall again). I think her uncontrollable temper was her mind's way of trying to shed this fake identity and stop denying the reality of the situation. She did not listen to her woman's intuition that told her the situation was not right, and her mind was speaking up for her. I am not defending her actions; however, therein lies a valuable lesson about repressing your feelings.

For the purpose of the case on *Cristina's Court*, she was the plaintiff, suing her ex-boyfriend for breaking into her house. He said he needed his work equipment and that he wasn't breaking in. He, in turn, was countersuing her for the broken Xbox and windshield. They were trying to put right what was broken, but what was broken was her self-identity, her self-esteem, and ultimately her reasons for reinventing herself for each chance at "love" that came along. You can't fix that in court.

I already touched briefly on the dangers of reinventing yourself for the wrong reasons, such as to avoid facing a problem or if you are looking for a quick fix to get out of a dull spot in your life or if you are looking for an instant remedy for feelings of fear or sadness. There is a growing demographic of women who are especially prone to wanting to reinvent themselves during times of frustration: single women. Even as a married woman, I know enough to realize that women who feel this way are everywhere.

Suddenly there do not seem to be enough single men to go around, and single women are exercising every available option they can think of to land that elusive Mr. Right. They are pleading with friends to be set up (it used to be that we shied away from blind dates for fear of how scary the unknown could be). I know this because I will admit that I have been known to play matchmaker for my single friends before. They are on every dating and social networking Web site imaginable, thinking that perhaps Mr. Right may just be in a different zip code. They are doing whatever it takes to find the man of their dreams. And in some cases, these women will succeed in these methods and find the love they are seeking.

In other cases, however, when all else appears to have failed, there are those who will decide that maybe if they pretend to be somebody else, they might increase their odds in the dating and relationship game. I am not talking about some sort of undercover, witness-protection disguise. I am talking about when frustrated single women decide to reinvent themselves in order to attract the man of their dreams. If this is not done correctly, however, it can lead to problems.

There is nothing wrong with wanting to improve yourself, but taking it to the extremes of adopting a new identity defeats the purpose. If you change the most authentic parts of your identity because you feel that they have somehow failed you in your search for the elusive perfect man (remember from the dating chapter that there is no such person), and you do meet him, then whom is he falling in love with? How can you be sure?

If you believe that you need to change some aspects of your identity to please or attract someone else, you are missing the point of reinvention. You should be working on who *you* want to be versus who you think others want you to be.

Remember, if you are not reinventing yourself from a place of self-confidence, happiness, acceptance of who you are, and security with your life, your reinvented self will reflect that and people will be able to see through it. I reminisced earlier in the book that the most important advice that my wonderful, wise executive producer of *Cristina's Court*, Peter Brennan, gave me before we taped the very first episode was to be myself, because if I was trying to be someone else, television viewers would see through my act immediately.

People are pretty savvy. They can sense when you are not being completely honest and authentic. It may not be a conscious piece of knowledge. They may just feel a sense of discomfort being around you. If you are reinventing yourself for the wrong reason, such as from the loneliness of being single, people's internal authenticity radars will start to pick it up. If your reinvented self does not come from a place of personal security and stability in your life, the most perfect companion for you in the world will not buy your act.

Ask yourself, How do you define yourself? If it is through the person you are with, the friends who validate you and make you feel popular, your money, or your job, then you need to dig deeper. Once you uncover those deeper layers, you will be able to tell the difference between the qualities that make you one-of-a-kind, and the things that you have outgrown. You will learn the difference between running away from your problems and moving ahead in your quest to improve yourself.

At the end of the day, know that however you choose to develop or reinvent yourself you are taking a powerful step that will help move you forward. Reinvention and self-development do not correct flaws or make up for past mistakes. When you reinvent yourself, you are nurturing the very best parts of your identity and growing as a person as a result. You are acknowledging the potential you have to create and shape your identity, without relying on the judgments or opinions of others.

Because as women we need to stop making excuses that we're not good enough. Who are you not good enough for, besides yourself? You are perfect in every way. No matter how you reinvent yourself, you will always be the best version of you that exists. When you make the choice to constantly look for ways to grow and evolve as a woman, you are honoring that.

My Verdict

Reinvention and self-development do not exist to make up for mistakes. What they do is present a golden opportunity to solidify and improve yourself and to keep expanding yourself and your identity. All reinvention needs to come from being present and making strong choices in the moment.

"IN HER OWN WORDS"

I asked some smart, confident women to share their thoughts on the laws covered in this chapter. Here is what they said, along with my responses.

Continued

How do you nurture your self-development?

1. "I call every Saturday 'Goddess Day,' and I spoil myself. This is by far one of the most important things I do for my career. It helps me gain perspective and gives me the energy I need for the following week. You can't pour water from an empty cup."

CP: See you Saturday! It's okay to take some time and give yourself permission to spoil yourself. Yet, after we finish spoiling ourselves we automatically look around without stopping to see what everyone else needs. Building on what she said about the empty cup, I will add that you have to put some gas in your own tank before leaving the driveway.

2. "To work on my own self-development, I read anything I can get my hands on, listen well, and stay involved in the community, at work and at school."

CP: Listening well is the key. When you are in tune with yourself, you will not make as many mistakes and you can better yourself.

Chapter 10

Law #10: *Live with It*

Every decision I make every single day, good and bad, I have to live with. We all do. As the days have passed, I have become more refined in my decision-making abilities, so hopefully the good decisions outnumber the bad ones. But honestly, I must admit that I learn more and become stronger from making bad decisions.

How often do we stop and reflect deeply on our good decisions? Good decisions yield good results, and we never give them a second thought. And yet when we make bad ones, we are prompted to put the brakes on and think about what happened—the consequences—and how to avoid repeating such decisions in the future. Bad decisions can be valuable learning experiences, but they should never be roadblocks to growth and self-development.

Making Smart Decisions

The first step to living with "it," with yourself, with your identity is learning to make decisions and not regretting them, even if they turn out to be mistakes. I have found that the best method of making decisions in life is by moving forward. This is a far more interesting and much faster way of seeing what is out there and making a choice you can live with than standing still and trying to find yourself. I have learned the most about myself as a person and had by far the most character-building adventures while I was taking action. Undecided about which direction you want to go in next with your life? Pick one. That's right—choose. At any given point in life there are countless options surrounding you as to where you can go and what you can do. You can either look at this as mass confusion or as a massive opportunity. And if you pick a path, go down it, and don't like it, most of the time you are perfectly free to pick a new direction.

There is, of course, a lot of value in being still, being alone with your thoughts, working on being present, and meditating. The danger is getting stuck there. Keep moving, and don't worry about making a wrong decision or making a wrong turn. Sometimes to find yourself you have to allow yourself to get lost in the first place.

Once you have found the courage to move forward and make a decision, you must find a way to be happy with it. I know this is a tough one, because as women we continuously analyze every high-heeled step we take. What it comes down to is that, as long as you have weighed the pros and cons of your decision, you have to dig deep and tap into the self-confidence that resides in us all, and make the choice to live with it without regret.

Even if some of your decisions turn out to be mistakes (after all, to err is human), find the confidence within yourself to accept that you are not perfect and that this happens to the best of us. Realize that it was not perhaps your brightest shining moment as a woman, *find the lesson* in it, and move on. It takes a lot of self-confidence and self-love to accept any bad decisions we have made. But instead of beating ourselves up for each bad decision, we need to zoom out and look at the overall tally. If you are okay with the majority of the choices you have made in your life, that should be enough to drive you forward to enjoy your life—the good, the bad, the ugly, and, of course, the beautiful.

The key to tilting that tally in your favor and making more good decisions than bad is to always make choices that are smart for you and reflect who you are. Make the choices that make you feel confident, that have the highest probability of creating success in your life, and that give you peace of mind. And by *you* I mean you, as in not everyone else around you. As much as I wish peace of mind for all my loved ones, I know that I am not responsible for creating it by making decisions that reflect what they think I should do. When you make the choices that reflect who you are and then make the choice to live with those decisions, that is sexy. This confidence creates an undeniable sense of self that no one can take away from you.

I have joked about Wonder Woman throughout the book, and all the false expectations the mere idea of her has placed on all our shoulders. But, in a way, we have been building our superhero identity throughout this book, one law at a time. We may not be *actual* superheroes, but we are each the best and most unique version of ourselves that is possible. Our true superpower is being able to live with this knowledge, along with the understanding that we cannot be perfect. We have to forgive ourselves and one another. Then we can look at the worst-case scenario and see that it has not happened. The key is to then move on and stop beating ourselves up.

We should not fear being weak when what we are is more powerful than most of us will ever realize. We need to stop getting paralyzed in the quest for a personal perfection that does not exist. There is no perfect person. Everyone is simply doing the best they can to be the best version of themselves.

Life is a struggle, so let's not fight the things that are trying to come naturally to us. If you are *still* questioning your own ability to succeed in life, perfect or not, without regret, remember, you have the unique ability to handle everything that lands on your plate, because it is meant for you and only you. Try to see your life as more of a natural flow of opportunities that will come naturally to you.

The Key to Living with It

You may be surprised to learn that *Cristina's Court* was filmed entirely in Houston, Texas. Since I live in Los Angeles with my family, this meant a hectic schedule of flying back and forth from Houston to Los Angeles every other week. Of course, I missed my family while we were apart, but I love the show and everyone involved.

Anyway, back to the matter of all those airline flights from time zone to time zone. If we turned back the hands of time to my younger self, the idea of traveling by myself on a regular basis would have been nothing less than awful. I used to hate doing things by myself. But now I see my frequent-flier time to and from work as my own special self-reflection time.

This self-realization certainly did not happen overnight. It was a gradual learning process finding out that I really do cherish time by myself, because it gives me time to think about the most important things in life and put them all in perspective. Sitting in my airplane seat, staring out the window at the big and often overwhelming world thirty thousand feet below, I often thought about how we women drive ourselves crazy with all the little things in life that we think have to be perfect. We agonize over every decision we have made—as if we have the power to turn back time and make the decision all over again, a different way. We worry that we somehow did something that resulted in our not having the biggest house, best car, most ideal job, or any of the other things that at some point in our lives we think are *so* important.

I looked out the airplane window through the clouds at all the houses below, imagining the women down there beating themselves up over past decisions. I wanted to tell all those women in all those houses that when we do this, and when we continuously fight our own perceived imperfections, all we are doing is robbing ourselves of contentment and self-fulfillment.

The little things we think have to be perfect and drive ourselves crazy over are not the essence of life—not even close. Life is not perfect and neither are we. This is why I pick my battles and fight only for what is most important to me. That is how you assign value to your identity: by assigning meaning to *all* the pieces of yourself. *You* decide how important your family is, your career, your inner strength, your beauty, your age, your femininity, your strengths, your weaknesses, your friends, and everything else included in these laws.

When you assign importance—this potential for greatness and fulfillment—to all the things that matter most to you, suddenly you have gained a perspective like no other. You have stepped back and seen the big picture. You see that your decisions are, well, what they are. They're not perfect, because neither are you and neither is life. Your decisions paved the road that got you to this point in your life, for better or for worse. The only thing left is learning to live with the life you have created for yourself, and all the choices that made it what it is.

Accepting the life you have created starts with accepting who you are when you are by yourself. On my thirtieth birthday, when I found myself sitting alone at that big table, I found myself thinking about my newfound contentment in being comfortable alone. To enjoy being by yourself, you really have to like and value yourself. You also must invest all the things in a relationship with yourself that you invest in your friendships. Before you marry someone else, you have to be able to marry yourself, live with yourself, like and accept yourself. Learn the difference between missing your loved ones and being unable to be away from them. If your comfort zone is entirely rooted in the presence of other people, then it is time to step outside it. Because if you do not like or accept yourself, how can you form deep and lasting bonds with anyone else?

The point I am making is that *you* have to be the model for all the laws in this book. Wearing your strong identity starts with finding happiness and contentment within yourself and the choices you make. Then you will have created a strong, secure, grounded identity to bring into all those other areas of your life. It starts with learning to be comfortable, happy, and fulfilled with nobody there but yourself. The core of being a smart, successful, and sexy woman is being so proud of and happy with *that* woman first.

People often ask me where I want to be ten years from now. Sometimes I get the feeling that they are looking for a big wish-list answer that encompasses bigger houses, more awards, more fame, and tons of money. My answer is a lot simpler: I want to be in the same situation I am in now, with things just a little better. I want the same love, the same good health, the same affections, and the same happiness. As long as I have that I know things will be better. That is the road I embark on every day of my life, and I know my choices reflect that. I have learned to live with my decisions and choices, because I know that when I make them, I am doing the very best I can—and that is the key to living with yourself in this moment.

In this moment all your decisions are good ones. In this moment you have not made any mistakes and have nothing to apologize for. In this moment you can live with your decisions, start fresh, and move forward again.

"In the moment" is quite possibly the last guilt-free zone that we women, notorious worriers, have to live in. I personally try to spend as much time there as possible—when I'm not allowing all of life's distractions to yank me out of it, of course. In the moment, I am empowered to make the decisions that honor who I am and what I want, without guilt. I make things happen instead of waiting for them to happen to me. It is impossible to worry about goals unmet and dreams unrealized, because every new moment is a new starting line. We must see each moment as a new opportunity to dream new dreams, and to set new goals and start moving closer to them, without looking in the rearview mirror at missed opportunities.

When you learn to live with the results of your decisions and the identity you have created, you learn to appreciate every moment of your life. Every morning when we wake up and get out of bed we unconsciously take for granted that we will climb back into bed again at the end of the day. This is not a given, of course. Rather than seeing this as fatalistic, see it as an opportunity to seize the day and be mindful of every moment you have on this earth.

There is nothing to be afraid of in this moment. Fears that we might never be able to live up to expectations are less of a reality now. In this moment it is easier to see the potential for greatness rather than failure or imperfection.

My Verdict

The most beautiful aspect of life is that it is not perfect. You are always on your toes, because no two days are the same, even the days with set schedules. Uncover that same imperfect beauty in yourself and discover your power to enjoy each day wearing the best version of your identity that you can.

"IN HER OWN WORDS"

I asked some smart, confident women to share their thoughts on the laws covered in this chapter. Here is what they said, along with my responses.

Continued

How do you live with your decisions?

1. "One of my weaknesses as a woman is not being a hundred percent present and in the moment. This is something I work on every day, because it is so important. Getting caught up in where I want to be and mistakes I have made is not being a hundred percent in this moment."

CP: This is one of our biggest weaknesses, trying to do everything in life and forgetting what we are doing right now. The solution is to look around and see what is *most* important to you and focus on that. Stop, look, and listen.

2. "I can let what people think about me spiral into a negative thought cloud at times."

CP: This is so true; it becomes a disease. Remember to take a step back from the situation, get perspective, and ask yourself how important what this person thinks of you will be five years from now.

3. "I'm getting better at this, but sometimes I will try to make myself feel better by pretending I never really wanted what I was going for in the first place."

CP: Denying your goals and what you want are negative things and hurt your identity in the long run. Part of achieving your goals is understanding that you will not always get them, but learning that maybe they were not actually what you needed right now. You have to understand that you did not get what you want for a reason, but you should *never* pretend that you did not want it at all.

PART V
Conclusion
The Empowered Identity

The laws I have laid out in this book have all, in their own way, identified various aspects of the sexy, smart, successful woman's identity. This is an extremely empowered identity to wear in life. An empowered woman knows how to find strength in herself, her purpose, and her opinion, and is aware of her downfalls while simultaneously working to improve herself every day. When you empower yourself as a woman you also recognize and accentuate some of the most beautiful parts of being a woman—femininity, body image, aging with grace, and natural beauty. An empowered woman is not afraid to take risks and step outside of her comfort zone, but is still strong enough to say no when it is right for her.

An empowered woman takes her unique identity with her into dating, marriage, and her friendships. She uses her understanding of who she is and what her priorities are to balance all the roles she plays in life, from home to the office and out in the community—and she makes it look effortless. An empowered woman has developed such a solid sense of who she is that she feels it in her gut when the time comes for personal change, self-development, and reinvention. And finally, no matter what choices and decisions she makes, the empowered woman knows how to take ownership of her actions, graciously forgive herself and others when forgiveness is necessary, and continue moving forward through life, knowing she is ready to handle what is around the next corner.

However, in order to define the identity of an empowered woman, we need to understand what forms the character at the heart of this identity. To me, it is being aware of your pros and cons, your strengths and weaknesses, your downfalls, and finding a way to celebrate who you are. It is understanding life and the rules of the game, and that life is not always fair. Character is a part of who you are—the person who has lived your life, made your mistakes, and experienced your triumphs. That is who you need to be proud of and portray in every moment.

And you don't need to scream it and force it on the world either. Because, as women, we don't always have to be the loudest. We do not have to yell our way through the glass ceiling. We can speak with a soft, feminine confidence and have a powerful impact. We can also make mistakes without fear, because we know that this is a risk taken when living life outside of our comfort zone.

We do not have to be scared every time we stumble that we will forget to get up, dust ourselves off, and keep going. A woman with good character shows strength when it is the hardest. There are women in this world who do this as a way of life. If you still do not see how strong we are as women, whether we are trying to be or not, look at the strongest ones among us for inspiration. Look at the women trying to survive in impoverished countries or in war zones, and even those among us here in our country who share the common goal—the womanly instinct—of caring for their family in the face of any imaginable hardship. These are women who show strength when it is the hardest and when the odds of triumph seem slim. Yet they find the resilience within themselves in the worst of circumstances, and they soldier on.

As women we have an unbelievable collective soul. We have all the emotion, the desire, the strength, and the passion to move mountains when we put our minds to it. Yet sometimes the effort seems beyond our capabilities. We listen to the rumors that state we are "just women" and slink into the corner, believing that our desires are much greater than our talents.

I would hope that the collection of life lessons, observations, and stories in this book have proven the exact opposite to you. The only things holding back our talents and untapped potential are fear and self-doubt.

Now, as we part ways, the best final piece of advice I can give you is to find that circle of strength in your own life. It is there, all around you, and hopefully the stories of the people in my circle will help you identify yours. The people in your circle have seen the best in you. They know why your identity is a unique one, and they are obviously attracted to it.

As I said in the beginning, each one of us wears her identity in a different way. There is no wrong way to be yourself. So why would you want to be anything except strong, sexy, smart, and successful?

The Final Verdict

I have found that when you are trying to see the big picture and learn the most all-encompassing lessons, the best thing to do is put together the puzzle pieces. Because it can be a rough world out there, especially if you let self-doubt be your best friend and worst enemy. Being true to yourself means knowing who you are, accepting your downfalls, and celebrating your strengths. It is all about depending on, trusting, and forgiving yourself. That is what makes you strong and leads you to make smart decisions on your own behalf.

And a strong woman who makes smart decisions knows how to be comfortable with who she is and in the body that God gave her. She knows that this is a trait of an empowered woman that reflects the kind of quiet confidence in herself that exudes grace and inner strength. She will be the first to remind you that the beauty and simplicity of life is being proud of who *you are*—and being who *you* are is sexy.

There is nothing sexier than the power that comes from knowing when to say no. Because *no* is a powerful word. It can be debilitating but also liberating. Knowing the difference means allowing your courage to guide you. Life is an ongoing education, and the best way to advance from level to level is to keep taking chances and learn to live outside your comfort zone.

For some women, the mere idea of dating is outside their comfort zone, because dating is an unpredictable journey that never follows the script from your fantasies. Nevertheless, throughout the trials and tribulations of finding the man who is perfect for you, remember this: A strong woman has faith in herself.

She knows before engaging her heart to be sure that her head is already in gear. Know what you know, do not deny the obvious, and realize that when you say, "I do"—it's for real.

Once you really do say, "I do," you learn that a good marriage is one that allows each partner to have the complete freedom to be individuals, together yet separate. In marriage, becoming a "we" is not a bad thing at all—as long as you do not lose your "I."

I remember an inspiring group of individuals called the Dukes. They made their friends into family and kept that family together, even after the Duke named Pee Wee passed on. The story of the Dukes shows that friendship is a valuable gift that is not freely given, but must be earned. It should never be taken for granted, and, for the lucky ones, it lasts a lifetime.

During that lifetime, there is much work to be done as we juggle our marriage and friendships. Even Wonder Woman would find it challenging to balance all the roles, responsibilities, and priorities that we real-life women face in our lives. Fortunately, instead of magic wristbands and an invisible plane, we have strength of spirit and the knowledge in our hearts that *we can do it.*

Even with the confidence that we can do it, when we stumble or even trip and fall, we know that reinvention and self-development do not exist to make up for mistakes. What they do is present a golden opportunity to solidify and improve yourself and to keep expanding yourself and your identity. All reinvention needs to come from being present and making strong choices in the moment.

From moment to moment, the most beautiful aspect of life is that it is not perfect. You are always on your toes, because no two days are the same, even the days with a set schedule. Uncover that same imperfect beauty in yourself, and discover your power to enjoy each day wearing the best version of your identity that you can.

With Thanks

This book would not have been possible without the broad and generous cooperation of many people, most particularly Christine Whitmarsh, my friend with "superpowers." I am also deeply indebted to my many friends (men and women alike) for their invaluable contributions. A special thank-you to the most genuine and selfless professionals and human beings I have ever met: Peter Brennan, executive producer of *Cristina's Court,* and Lisa Lew, supervising producer of *Cristina's Court.* Their friendship and mentorship have been a very special part of my life. Working with Peter and Lisa and being friends with them has given me valuable life lessons that I will forever cherish. As always, I express my enduring gratitude to my friend and agent Eric Rovner and the entire William Morris Endeavor Entertainment team. And a heartfelt thanks to everyone at Penguin Books, with a special appreciation to Raymond Garcia and Kim Suarez.